STEVEN
SPIELBERG

D1178151

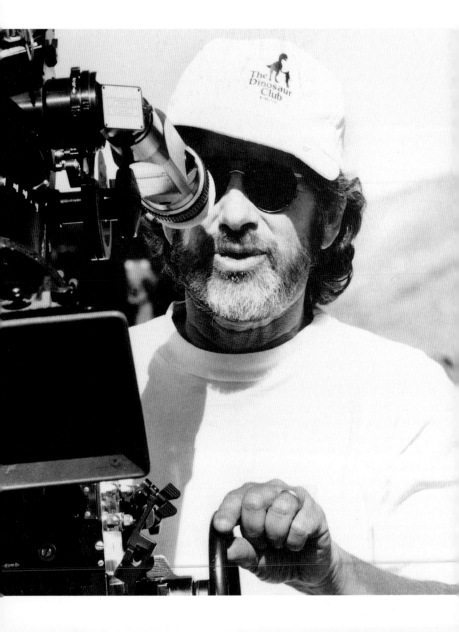

STEVEN SPIELBERG

George Perry

ORION

First published in 1998 by Orion Media
An imprint of Orion Books Ltd
Orion House, 5 Upper St Martin's Lane, London WC2H 9EA

Project editor: Natasha Martyn-Johns
Designed by Leigh Jones

All illustrations supplied by Photofest,
The Kobal Collection, Pictorial Press Ltd.

A CIP catalogue record for this book is available
from the British Library.

Printed and bound in Italy

CONTENTS

1 Does He Know Something?

Out over the Pacific a memorable sunset was developing, flushing the sky with a vivid magenta, violet and saffron glow. The southern Californian coast often enjoys great sunsets but this was one so stunningly beautiful that it brought the joggers and the rollerskaters at Venice and Santa Monica to a standstill as they gaped, awed by its spectacle. Further up the littoral a man sat in solitude on the quieter sandy shore of Malibu. He too spent several minutes staring at the remarkable natural phenomenon, no doubt admiring the quality of nature's own special effects department. Eventually he got up and went to his nearby home. At which point another man, who had been watching the other unobserved, swiftly moved to settle himself on the sand in exactly the same spot, continuing the gaze out over the ocean where the sun had long since vanished, leaving only the fading streaks in the sky.

The first man was Steven Spielberg, then near his apogee as the most successful film-maker Hollywood had ever known. The other man was an anonymous producer, a fringe inhabitant of the Malibu movie colony, who had been hoping that by some curious osmotic effect something of the vision that had driven Spielberg would enter his own psyche. In the Hollywood community the seven deadly sins flourish rather more than in most of small-town America, and envy is usually near the head of the list. The story may not necessarily be true, although I have heard it from two separate sources, but as an illustration of the way Spielberg is perceived it is apt. And in an instance of the way myths develop, the British film monthly *Empire*, in its issue of March 1998, updated an amended version of the incident to the summer of 1993, naming the interloper as Mark Canton, who was at the time the chairman of Sony. Having first told this particular anecdote in *The Sunday Times* in 1986 I was amused that the fable had, as showbiz lingo has it, legs.

The screenwriter William Goldman in his book *Adventures in the Screen Trade*, one of the shrewdest insider's views on the curious process of making movies, said that the single most important fact that prevails in the industry is that 'Nobody knows anything.' No matter how high his salary, or generous his stock options, even the most powerful studio executive has no more idea of which pictures are going to click with the public than does his own office cleaner. The direction of Spielberg's extraordinary career suggests that he was a being who really did know something, a rare gift, whether acquired by necromancy or intuition. It seems that in some miraculous way he has a private line on public taste. Only a handful of the dominant figures in the history of Hollywood have been so blessed, and even then not consistently throughout their entire careers. Certainly Walt Disney would qualify for membership of this exclusive club, and so would Alfred Hitchcock, who knew more than anybody how the merest frisson of fear could supercharge an audience's sense of anticipation. But few others.

With the success of *Jaws* in 1975 Steven Spielberg ascended into the stratosphere of box-office directors, and when *Close Encounters of the Third Kind*, *Raiders of the Lost Ark*, *ET The Extra-Terrestrial*, *Jurassic Park* and *Schindler's List* are added to the roster it can be seen that his record for creating megahits is unmatched, even though he has officially directed only sixteen films. He has also been a catalytic force within the industry, acquiring and nurturing fresh talents and sponsoring his contemporaries in the production of films under the Amblin Entertainment and later, for *Amistad* and *Saving Private Ryan*, DreamWorks banners. The movie brat of the 1970s has, by the late 1990s, become an elder statesman, a position sanctioned and recognized by the Hollywood establishment in the 1994 Academy Awards, when the Oscars that had so eluded him in earlier years came in a deluge for *Schindler's List*. The precocious success of his earlier films had aroused jealousy, suspicion and unease. It was as though he was being punished for trying too hard, yet his work was influential to the point of shameless imitation by those who pretended to be indifferent. In reality it is arguable that his influence on the American film of his day been as definitive as that of Griffith in his own time, although his detractors would probably hate to admit it.

It is not always the case that a capability for generating gigantic box-office grosses with the production of artistically valid films go together. There are any number of high-revenue producing movies, such as James Cameron's bloated epic *Titanic*, that cannot be regarded as anything more than slick crowd-pleasers, and sometimes they have little lasting merit. There is indisputably a recognizable signature on all of Spielberg's films, which, although often imaginatively conceived, are invariably directed in a solid, craftsmanlike way, carefully observing essential film grammar with a skill that seems positively old-fashioned when compared with the manic riffs of Oliver Stone or the frenetic pacing of Quentin Tarantino. Spielberg prepares meticulously – rewriting, story-boarding, editing in advance. The authority of Spielberg's work stems from the thoroughness with which he embraces his cinematic education although, contrary to the popular myth that he is the most illustrious alumnus from a film-school background, he is in the main self-taught.

Hollywood's greater directors have recognizable characteristics, trademarks that signify their authorship and provide the public with the thrill of expectation. Thus Hitchcock was the master of suspense, Capra the arch-populist with a whimsical twist, Wilder the astringent cynic, Ford the creator of an elegiac Western mythology, Cukor the exponent of sophisticated feminine drama, Preston Sturges the blender of screwball comedy and small-town satire, Wyler the careful craftsman of grand themes. Spielberg actually has an approach more in common with these, his own heroic figures of past glories of cinema, than with his immediate peers, even though they include Martin Scorsese, Francis Coppola, Brian De Palma and John Milius, all of them as cine-literate as himself. His personal defining note that recurs throughout much of his work is a sense of wonder, almost a childlike perception of the infinity of possibilities, distinctly tangible in his science-fiction fantasies such as *Close Encounters*, *ET The Extra-Terrestrial* and *Jurassic Park*, but also discernible in his serious dramas of oppression, *The Color Purple*, *Empire of the Sun*, *Schindler's List* and *Amistad* where, in the face of apparently hopeless odds, the free human spirit ultimately triumphs. Film-makers such as Stone and Tarantino take a pessimistic view of human nature, seeing an ingrained capability to mess things up as part of the treachery of mankind. In comparison with them Spielberg is a sunny optimist, with a positively old-fashioned belief in redemption. Even such a monster as Amon Goeth in *Schindler's List* has a moment of atonement before he meets his fate.

Spielberg's critics have often accused him of taking too simplistic a view, of never having really grown up enough to understand that misery is an endemic condition of the human tragedy, and that his uplifting, hopeful conclusions are a betrayal of the truth, all in the interests of good box office. Spielberg likes to round off his films properly without the loose ends flapping in the wind and, if it means that he is giving his audiences an affirmative note to depart with into the night, it has both served him well in the appreciation shown to him in the form of astonishing box-office receipts, and clearly satisfied his own instincts. The bleakest ending to a Spielberg film is not that of the cemetery scene in *Schindler's List* or even *Amistad*, when a title reveals that Cinque, having endured so much in attaining his freedom and repatriation to his African home-land, learns that his wife and child have vanished, almost certainly sold off to slave traders. The bleak moment, the notable, almost singular exception is *Poltergeist*, which although it was credited to Tobe Hooper, was so closely supervised by Spielberg that it can be regarded as his film, where a suburban family is destroyed by paranormal forces that inhabit their newly-built home.

Spielberg has a natural affinity with children, and is a father or step-father to seven in his own family. His ability to draw young minds towards his work has often been compared with those remarkable instincts of Walt Disney, who also knew that children are far more resilient when it comes to fear than most adults appreciate. The attack by a *Tyrannosaurus rex* on the youngsters in *Jurassic Park* had adults cowering in their seats, but was relished by the junior members of the audience. Even the most anodyne of Disney films contains moments of terror. Certain elements of *Snow White and the Seven Dwarfs* prompted the London County Council to impose an A certificate, prohibiting children to see it without an adult. A few years ago after I had visited Spielberg in Los Angeles he sent me a signed photograph of himself that had been requested by my son, then aged nine but already able to quote verbatim chunks of dialogue from *ET The Extra-Terrestrial*, and the message he addressed to him was, 'Imagination is the key to our future.' A pompous injunction to a nine-year-old? Not at all. He was identifying the driving characteristic of the achiever. Or to put an embroidery on the phrase *cogito ergo sum*, his philosophy is I think therefore I can do.

Any analysis of Spielberg's work has to understand the source from which his motivation derives, the personal circumstances of his upbring-ing and development that led him on the path to attaining and sustain-ing his pole position on the Hollywood grid. There has been in recent years a spate of biographies of him, a sign that at last the prejudices against admitting him into the inner circle are fading, and it will be necessary to recapitulate some of the facts as the celluloid career is examined.

2 The Boy Wonder

Steven Allan Spielberg was born in the Jewish Hospital, Cincinnati, Ohio, on 18 December 1946. It is a disputed date; the usually reliable *Film Encyclopedia* by Ephraim Katz gives the year as 1947, but the confusion is understandable, since Spielberg himself later trimmed a year off his age, a practice not unknown in the film business, and particularly useful to him at the brink of his career when he was anxious to feed the *wunderkind* image that was helping his progress. The evidence of the birth certificate is however irrefutable.

His parents, both of whom are still alive, were somewhat dissimilarly talented. His father Arnold was an electrical engineer at a GE plant, an occupation that required frequent uprooting, and a move of perhaps hundreds of miles to another area, followed for their son by a new school and the need to establish fresh friendships. His mother Leah was a concert pianist, and doted on him, in comparison with his more restrained father. From Cincinnati the family moved to Haddonfield, New Jersey, and then on to Arizona, first to Arcadia, and next to Scottsdale, the plushy suburb of Phoenix, where he spent most of his childhood with his three younger sisters until the age of sixteen. It was perhaps unfortunate that this middle-class, although not overtly devout, Jewish family should choose to live in what was then a virtually enclosed and exclusive WASP neighbourhood, and that at holiday times such as Christmas the Spielberg's Jewishness would be all too apparent, as theirs would be the only home not to be festooned with elaborate decorations. At school the young Steven was often taunted for being a Jew, in the mindless juvenile anti-Semitism that was similar to the pillorying of other kids because they were fat or spotty. It was upsetting enough for him to attempt his own corrective surgery on his nose by applying adhesive tape.

He has often recalled that the first film he saw was Cecil B. DeMille's *The Greatest Show on Earth*, which was released in 1952, although he believes that it was in the following year that he went to watch it, accompanied by his father, during a visit to Philadelphia. The child's initial disappointment, when he discovered that the circus he thought that he was going to see was not a real one, was assuaged by the lavish spectacle on screen, which included a cataclysmic train wreck. Later he became entranced by Disney cartoons, particularly the full-length features. The boy was not a great mixer, and was a bundle of neuroses. Unsurprisingly as the television age made headway he became an addict, watching from *Howdy Doody*, through to *Your Show of Shows* with Sid Caesar, and on to *The Honeymooners* with Jackie Gleason, and eventually when the station closed down, the test card, all with the connivance of his babysitter. Television was then still a novelty and its social implications had still not been formally appreciated. For a youth who found his schoolmates not only over-athletic, but driven by their ingrained anti-Semitic prejudice, the box in the corner was an agreeable surrogate companion.

At the age of twelve the idea that he could become a film-maker actually took hold. He had been experimenting for some time with his father's 8mm Kodak camera, having taken control of the family home-movies department after his constant criticism of his parent's shaky camera work and poor composition. He began to make edited versions of their weekend camping trips into the rugged Arizona wilderness, and it was not long before the boy began to make up his own short stories for the camera. From there it was a logical next step to write a script and to cast schoolfriends in parts. It was also a way of overcoming his unpopularity, which dwindled away when other children appreciated that he was good at something that they themselves could not do.

The first film came about as a Boy Scout proficiency test, in order to win his photographer's badge. Normally, still photography was all that was required, but the eager young Spielberg was able to convince his scoutmaster to accept a movie. The exhilarating three-minute result, a silent without inter-titles, was a cod-western taking as its prototype the then popular television series *Gunsmoke*, and came complete with a stagecoach hold-up (filmed so that the absence of horses would not be noticeable) and the robber getting his desserts by being thrown from a cliff, calling for ingenious in-camera special effects. After that there was no problem in acquiring the coveted badge.

He had also become an exhibitor, renting first 8mm and later 16mm films which he would show to the other neighbourhood children on Saturday afternoons in the family living room. The cost of the rental would be met by a small admission charge and, in a prescient touch, the sale of ten-cent bags of popcorn. Others in the family would help with the organization. His commercial instinct was shrewd, and already an ability to make money from his enthusiasms was beginning to form; the profits were ploughed back into production. He also raised money for local causes, and his altruism earned admiring attention in the local press, making it a worthwhile investment in publicity terms. He became a collector of films and soundtracks, and began studying them closely. His musical mother saw to it that he played the clarinet in the school band, but although he was a competent musician, it was his passion for movies that took precedence. So much so that in some teaching circles it was regarded as prejudicial to his general education. Then as now, his visual and aural senses were more powerful than his facility to interpret the printed page. Spielberg has invariably preferred to see a movie rather than read a book.

When he was in the seventh grade he began making a film with a World War Two setting, a fifteen-minute epic called *Fighter Squad*, which incorporated bits of stock footage of dogfights, and a vintage aircraft which he filmed at a nearby airport, ingeniously shooting it to look as if it was airborne. His juvenile mastery of editing, and judicial manipulation of close-up images was, from contemporary accounts, impressively precocious. His talents received attention from a Phoenix TV station in 1961 when he shot a forty-minute World War II film on a lost-patrol theme called *Escape to Nowhere* in the Camelback Mountain area, an ambitious work which he had begun two years earlier and did not finish until the following year. His 8mm film, enacted by youths of his own age in various makeshift uniforms, causing state troopers to enquire what the blazes all these adolescents were doing, roaming the highways in Nazi helmets, won the top prize in a state amateur film contest, the adjudicators noting that the special effects were astonishingly mature.

When he was sixteen, his parents separated, later to divorce, after several years of acute stress. They had moved from Phoenix to California, but after the split his mother and sisters returned to Arizona. He was now closer to the seat of the movie industry, and recalled some years later how he visited a Burbank sound stage during the filming of *PT–109*. He also made his first feature film, using as equipment a superior Bolex 8mm camera that he obtained by trading his *Escape to Nowhere* prize. He also was able for the first time to use sound. The script of his work, which was called *Firelight*, was carefully constructed visually although the dialogue was less compelling, and dealt with the appearance of mysterious objects in the skies above a fictitious Arizona town. It was a prodigious undertaking for a teenager, and perhaps served as therapy during the break-up of his parents' marriage. The similarities with his later *Close Encounters of the Third Kind* are marked. It also ensured that by the time he arrived in California he was already completely committed to the film world, and that his progress into the professional industry was only a matter of time. In the vacation preceding his senior year at Saratoga High School, near San Jose, he went down to Los Angeles and worked unpaid at Universal, ostensibly as an assistant in the editorial department, but he also used the opportunity to make extensive contacts and to bring attention to his work, particularly *Firelight*, which impressed a number of the old pros on the lot. He roamed the sound stages and watched the processes of film-making at close hand, as well as running useful errands for his nominal employers. He repeated the experience the following year. A myth later developed, partly from his own fancy, that he took over an empty office, had his name inscribed on the door and somehow infiltrated the system to the extent that others assumed that he was a very young studio executive. What, however, is true is that as a teenager he made the most of his chances to observe some of the foremost people in cinema in the process of creation, and was able to further his film education far more effectively than by learning theory in an academic environment.

Nevertheless, he wanted to attain such credentials. An attempt to enrol in the film school of the University of California, Los Angeles (UCLA) was abortive owing to his failure to achieve an A on graduation from high school. He was, however, to find a place at the somewhat less renowned California State College at Long Beach, which did not have a film school as such, but touched on the medium through its department of radio and television. In any case Spielberg had to major in English Literature, which was hardly his forte.

Unsurprisingly his college period, although it ensured that he was not drafted, was undistinguished academically, and he never graduated with a degree. However, he used the time to make more films, eventually putting together his first professional work, *Amblin'*, which was shot in the summer of 1968. The likes of Coppola and Scorsese were already making proficient student films at their respective schools and acquiring national publicity, as Hollywood awaited the time to come when they would start banging on the doors. Spielberg, in his lesser Long Beach surroundings, had already begun his apprenticeship earlier at Universal, and in certain respects was now ahead, in that he had a practical knowledge of studio workings and an invaluable range of contacts. Using them, he was able to spend three days a week at Universal even while he was taking classes, and would often shake down and sleep in an empty office to avoid the long drive. When not watching feature films being shot, or hanging around the cutting rooms talking to editors, he would take an interest in the production of television series that were already accounting for much of the work on the Universal lot. He claimed later to have worked on some of them, including *Wagon Train*. He also spent most of whatever time he had to spare viewing movies, often venturing into the obscure revival houses that could still be found in parts of Los Angeles.

The producer of *Amblin'* was Denis C. Hoffman, the proprietor of a company that made optical shots and titles in Hollywood. There are, even if to the outsider it seems incredible, stout-hearted characters who want to be film producers. Hoffman's investment did not stretch to a salary for Spielberg, and he retained a lien on his future for a further film. In the event it never happened and many years later, in 1995, there was a lawsuit, the basis of which was that twenty years earlier when *Jaws* had been released to thundering acclaim Spielberg had wriggled out of the early contract on the grounds that he was a minor at the time he signed it, and consequently under Californian law it was invalid. Hoffman soon afterwards had accepted a buyout of $30,000, including the use of the title *Amblin'*, which Spielberg, dropping the apostrophe, used as the name of his own production company. In 1994 when the birth certificate revealed the discrepancy in Spielberg's birth date, and that he was a year older than previously thought, Hoffman renewed his claim for an option on his services, claiming that $33 million was a more realistic buy-out figure. Spielberg made a counter suit, and the case caused considerable astonishment, even in Hollywood where litigation is an active pursuit as commonplace as tennis.

The short feature *Amblin'*, all of twenty-six minutes, was Spielberg's calling card, an ambitious youth's demonstration of talent and a cry for attention. It was shot on location in southern California over ten days, the story simply consisting of a youth (Richard Levin) and a girl (Pamela McMyler) who are making their way from the Mojave desert to the Pacific by hitching rides. There is no dialogue, but plenty of music and moody shots of dust and sunlight, exciting audiences at various festivals at which it was shown. Spielberg himself later intimated a dislike of the work, regarding it as an extended Pepsi commercial, and has kept it hidden from public gaze. The pay-off of the storyline occurs when the girl finally discovers what it is that the boy has concealed in his guitar case, and which he is so reluctant to allow her to see. When they reach the ocean she takes a look and discovers within it a business suit, polished shoes and an Arthur C. Clarke paperback. And all the time she had thought that he was a genuine hippy.

In many respects the idea was not particularly original, and there had been a vogue of middle-class rebellious youth taking to the desert high-ways in the search for whatever, most notably Antonioni's bloated American work, *Zabriskie Point*. Spielberg's little film went to some trouble to examine the characters and their interreaction, and the editing was smooth and assured, qualities that should have evoked favourable responses from those studio executives who actually saw it. Chuck Silvers, the film librarian at Universal, and his first studio friend, claimed that not only did it demonstrate the young Spielberg's instinctive understanding of where to position the camera, the test by which any director can stand or fall, but that the film moved him to tears.

Somehow Silvers persuaded Sidney Sheinberg, the dynamic head of television production at Universal, to take a look at it. It turned out to be the decisive move in the inauguration of Spielberg's career, since the thirty-three-year-old executive immediately responded to the work, and asked to see its young originator. Unfazed by Spielberg's appearance, which was that of a college-boy nerd, he offered him the chance to make a few television films, arguing that if his work was successful, it would be a useful springboard into features. The trust that Sheinberg showed in an untried but promising newcomer conditioned Spielberg's future outlook, and is often regarded as the prime reason why he has subsequently started off so many careers in others, exercising a similar faith in the ability of the individuals concerned to deliver.

Just before Christmas 1968 *Amblin'* had its première public performance, supporting an unfortunate Otto Preminger film, *Skidoo*. At that time of the year programming of Los Angeles cinemas is often adventurous and wide-ranging as so many films are rushed out to play for a statutory week in order to qualify for Academy Award consideration. Spielberg, just turned twenty-two, although generally assumed to be twenty-one, found that one or two of the reviews that appeared for the Preminger film had mentioned his briefly, but favourably. But further theatre bookings were difficult to achieve, the twenty-six-minute length proving awkward, although it was screened at festivals, winning an award at Atlanta, and Spielberg hoped that it would at least achieve a nomination for the best live-action short subject Academy Award. It did not, and was the first of many occasions when he felt the cold snub of the Academy.

He dropped out of California State after one semester of his junior year and started full-time work at Universal on $275 a week. His first assignment was to direct a segment of *Night Gallery*, a three-part television movie, in which three odd yarns by Rod Serling were linked, portmanteau fashion. It was to be the pilot for a series. The prolific, chain-smoking Serling, the producer-writer who at the start of his earlier famous series used to hove into view and announce that the evening's protagonist had just entered *The Twilight Zone*, was by now on the verge of being burned out. The glossy production values of *Night Gallery* with its big sets and luscious colour made the hokiness of the plotting, which had been an element of *The Twilight Zone*'s appeal, look painfully threadbare. Spielberg was plunged in at the deep end. It turned out that the episode he was to direct would have as its star a great screen diva, Joan Crawford, who like Serling was also nearing the end of her career. So desperate was she for the $50,000 fee that she had not even hesitated to replace her rival, Bette Davis, who had withdrawn after taking exception to the prospect of being directed by someone who looked like a college boy. Crawford was quite unaware. She played an immensely wealthy, reclusive, blind Manhattanite, the sole occupant of a luxurious penthouse in an apartment building which she owns. She blackmails a doctor into transplanting the eyes of a pathetic small-time crook who needs a quick infusion of cash which he owes. The operation is experimental and can

Spielberg's first assignment for Universal was to direct Joan Crawford in a segment of Night Gallery**, a three-part television movie.**

give her only a few hours in which to see, but she regards it as worth it just for a glimpse of trees and sunlight. The operation is carried out, and the moment comes when all by herself in her apartment she slowly removes the bandages. At the same moment that they come off the great blackout, which plunged the eastern seaboard of the United States into darkness in 1965, occurs. Believing the operation a failure, she stumbles around on a staircase, apparently even reaching the basement level, before returning to her apartment and falling asleep in her chair. When she awakes it is morning, and she sees the sunrise, but her brief time for having eyesight is over and as she watches it fades away. In an attempt to get closer to the light she plunges through a window and falls to her death.

As a screenplay it is so riddled with crass inconsistencies that even given the usual Serling line of fantasy it hardly passes muster. Why have her few hours of sight been timed to coincide with night-time when she has clearly asked to be able to see daylight? Why are no car headlights, emergency flares and battery standby lights visible in the blacked-out city? Why does she stumble helplessly in the darkness, something no blind person would ever do? How does she fall out of the window, which has mysteriously cracked and shatters when she touches it? And most pertinently, how could such laughable nonsense be seriously considered as fit to be put before the public? The last question, unfortunately, informs a considerable percentage of all Hollywood output at all times, and so nothing much has changed.

Spielberg was aware of the ludicrous nature of the story, but in his position was unable to do anything about it. His task was to get it filmed. As a vehicle for a neophyte director it served its purpose. Crawford, rather surprisingly, played her role with a certain subtlety, even offering an echo of one of her earlier 'unmasking' triumphs, the plastic surgeon's victory over her scars in Cukor's *A Woman's Face* in 1943, a film of which the movie-buffish Spielberg would almost certainly have been aware. After her initial surprise and discomfiture at his youthfulness they eventually hit it off, and she responded with confidence to his direction, although she had difficulty with her lines and occasionally had to be shown cue cards. Spielberg generally used fluid camera movements, including dolly and crane shots during dialogue which was unusual for a television movie. The two-day overrun on the seven-day schedule was not entirely his fault, since his star had become ill with an ear infection and needed a day off to recuperate. Another director might have accelerated the shooting rate, cutting corners to catch up, but that was not, and still is not the Spielbergian style. But his unorthodox shooting manner was unpopular, and he was excluded from the editing stage, when many of his more ambitious shots were replaced by conventional alternatives. The old hands were of the view that there was no place on network television for anything experimental, and that his gimmicky stuff belonged instead to art-house fare. An optical effect of his, called a spiral wipe, was retained, but the montage to denote the operation, consisting of two pairs of eyes, and the rotating image in Crawford's fall were both added by another hand. Spielberg solved the problem of portraying his leading figure in pitch darkness by lighting her against a matt-black background so that the only illumination appeared to come from herself. It was visually effective. The Spielberg episode of *Night Gallery* did not have an occult element, unlike the two others that book-ended his in the completed cut, which was first aired on 8 November 1969 on NBC, apparently with sufficient success to justify a three-year run for a *Night Gallery* series.

Meanwhile Spielberg found that his extreme youth and his penchant for fancy camera work had rendered him almost an outcast, and although he went on submitting ideas for further projects they were all turned down. Among them was a story elaborated from an incident in Texas that he had seen reported in a newspaper, in which an ex-convict and his wife had taken a highway patrolman hostage in an attempt to gain access to his children, who were in the custody of his father-in-law. It was, of course, the basis of his film *The Sugarland Express*, which was made four years later, but at the time that he first proposed it the studio was completely unenthusiastic.

Spielberg went on leave from Universal and entered a frustrating period, attempting to raise money for independent features and to collaborate with other would-be film-makers. He received a screen credit for the story of *Ace Eli and Rodger of the Skies*, in which Cliff Robertson played a barnstorming pilot, but could not persuade Twentieth Century Fox to allow him to direct it. Back at Universal he made an episode of *Marcus Welby, MD*, which was followed by episodes for other series, including, as it happened, as well as *The Name of the Game*, *The Psychiatrist*, *Owen Marshall, Counsellor at Law* and *Columbo*, with Peter Falk. He had learned to play the television game, and developed a constructive technique that managed to get the job done within the appropriate time frame without making too many creative compromises. He also earned the respect of his crews, who appreciated that in spite of his uninspiring appearance he had an instinctive grasp of film-making, and was prepared to listen. The work kept him busy, even though he was biding his time to make the leap into features.

His episode, 'LA 2017', for *The Name of the Game* series came closer than any of his other television work in foreshadowing the direction in which he was travelling. Set in a future Los Angeles so polluted that its citizenry are obliged to live underground, it anticipated *Logan's Run* and *Blade Runner*, and earned praise from television critics for its effects and the impact of its ecological message.

3 Devil in the Machine

A new assignment for Spielberg was to direct an *ABC Movie of the Week* called *Duel*, his closest yet to a film proper. The subject was taken from a story by the science-fiction writer Richard Matheson, who had been responsible for many memorable episodes of *The Twilight Zone*. It had appeared in the April 1971 issue of *Playboy*, and describes an epic struggle on a western highway between a car driver and an awesomely malevolent truck. Universal had bought the story and Matheson had produced a screenplay in conjunction with George Eckstein, who was a producer on *The Name of the Game*. It found its way into Spielberg's hands and immediately he saw its possibilities, and started to come up with ideas on how to shoot it, even though other directors had declared that it presented too many difficulties. Their reservations were based on the premise that the car driver is pitted against an enemy, the truck driver, who has no presence at all, the opaque windows hiding him completely, so that it is his vehicle that becomes the enemy. For that reason it was not even regarded as a contender for theatrical release, the judgement being that there were too few elements in it to grab and hold an audience's attention.

Given a sixteen-day shooting schedule, and a location that had to be rugged, remote and yet for budget reasons close enough to Los Angeles to enable everybody involved to live at home, Spielberg was obliged to work fast. The casting of the truck as a character was as propitious as having as his lead Dennis Weaver, always remembered by film buffs for his portrayal of the terrified motel clerk in Orson Welles's *Touch of Evil*, playing its opponent, a road-bound minor businessman with an unhappy, dissatisfied wife back home. The truck was a well-used, beaten-up Peterbilt tanker, distressed further by being given a bad paint job in streaky brown and black. Its driver was never to be seen, and so the windows were rendered impenetrable beneath a film of dust and impacted insects. The location site was a fifteen-mile stretch of California state highway 14, a forty-five-minute drive to the north of Los Angeles, and Spielberg carefully surveyed the road to find as many angles as possible to avoid repetition.

Weaver had not been Spielberg's choice, and the actor found it difficult to accept the way that the character was interpreted, as a weak-
willed, troubled, defensive, neurotic member of the middle underclass.
He was mistaken. That reading was far more satisfactory than had
Spielberg given him a conventionally assertive, macho, defiant posture.
His indignant reaction when the truck first begins its aggressive tactics
on the highway echoes realistically the feelings of most ordinary people
finding themselves in similar situations, and as the attacks become ever
more menacing and potentially lethal, sympathy swings towards him.
Eventually the viewer becomes so consumed by the escalation of the
action that Weaver's final triumph, in managing to lure the truck over a
cliff to its destruction, an act that in real life could be construed as
murder, is greeted with sighs of relief. Good has vanquished evil. The
devil in the machine has been destroyed. There have probably been no
better attempts to capture the lunatic irrationality of road rage in a film.

The battle between the truck and the car begins gradually, as the fume-
belching tanker hogs a winding mountain road, callously preventing the
smaller vehicle from passing. It develops into a cat-and-mouse exercise,
and at one point Weaver finds himself waved on to move ahead, only to
discover almost too late that he is making for a head-on collision with
traffic coming the other way. Spielberg punctuates the road jockeying
with interludes such as the destruction of a roadside snake farm when
the truck drives round it in frenzied circles, demolishing the reptiles'
containers and creating yet more danger for Weaver. At another point it
attempts to push Weaver's car onto a railroad track along which a freight
train is rapidly looming.

Spielberg used inventive cinematography in conjunction with Jack A.
Marta, who was the director of photography. Wide-angle mounts emphasized the menacing bulk of the truck and the puny frailty of the car. Hand-
held shots from the car's interior vividly conveyed Weaver's panic as he
manipulates the wheel. The director revealed in a talk to an audience at
the National Film Theatre, London, that he himself was visible in some
shots, but only in the projected theatrical form, and not on television.
When he edited he used the 1:33 aspect ratio of the television image and
so was unaware of what would show when a 1:85 print was struck.

Duel aired on 13 November 1971, accompanied by considerable pre-
publicity from Universal and the network, both suddenly aware that what
they were about to show was anything but a run-of-the-mill television
movie. It was decided to attempt a theatrical release overseas, and a new
cut increased the length from 73 minutes to 91 minutes. There have been
arguments that some of the tension is dissipated in the longer version
by showing Weaver's fraught domestic life. *Duel* could originally have
been a silent film, since normal dialogue is eschewed. The voice-over

narration, which was added against Spielberg's wishes in order to appease the dimmer members of the television audience, was modified, with an opening sequence in which Weaver listens to a radio phone-in during the long drive out of Los Angeles, while at the same time worrying about his wife who, when he phones her, is cool after what she considers was his offhandedness at a dinner party that took place on the previous evening. Another sequence that is in the extended version, but was not shown on television, is a curious encounter with a stranded school bus, its cargo of pupils distressed, in the middle of nowhere. The sinister truck suddenly goes out of character and pushes it along the road to get it restarted, temporarily suspending hostilities against Weaver. The notion of a school bus in peril was to recur in a later Spielberg film, *Always*, but here it feels like padding, adding unnecessarily to a taut drama, and essentially that is exactly what it is.

Before committing *Duel* to a circuit release in Britain the distributor arranged a special screening which was attended by the film critic of *The Sunday Times* in London, Dilys Powell, the British doyenne of the profession. She was impressed by what she saw, and encouraged her critical colleagues to see it. On the strength of her endorsement *Duel* was boosted out from its place in a suburban double bill and given greater prominence with a West End screening. It received widespread publicity, arousing curiosity as to what was so special about this film by an unknown. 'Mr Spielberg comes from television,' wrote Dilys Powell in her column after praising the subtle increase in tension and the varied pace and movement; 'he is only twenty-five. No prophecies; but somehow I fancy this is another name to look out for.' Spielberg always regarded her prescient, discerning judgement as an important factor in establishing him as a serious director. She died in 1995, and when her memorial service was held at St Martin-in-the-Fields later that year he sent a special message reiterating his gratitude. She had aroused the interest of the Olympian idols he admired, such as David Lean, who commented on his vision, and shrewdly added, 'But then Steven is the way movies used to be.'

When *Duel* was selected to be shown at the Cannes film festival Spielberg flew to Europe, his first trip from the United States, and was surprised to find that even though he arrived with no history he was regarded with some solemnity, and was puzzled and amused that Continental critics and other journalists insisted on interpreting the film in metaphorical terms that he had never for a moment considered. It was a valuable lesson. Many people in Hollywood make the mistake of seeing the rest of the world, particularly the English-speaking part, as an extension of the American market and fail to comprehend that taste and attitudes are often completely different. As early as this point in his career

Spielberg took on board that each territory has a unique perception and reaction, and he has subsequently always been wary of the European press. Nevertheless, in Europe *Duel* was a resounding success, and picked up a few prizes from festivals such as Avoriaz and Taormina.

He was now being offered films by other studios, but was unable to take them up, having been locked into a seven-year contract with Universal, and he was obliged to carry on providing material for television. Soon after finishing *Duel* he had made *Something Evil* for CBS, a horror story about demonic possession starring Sandy Dennis and Darren McGavin. During a frustrating period following *Duel*'s success he worked on several abortive projects, and made his last television film under the Universal contract. It was *Savage*, for NBC, in which Martin Landau played a television journalist uncovering a political blackmail plot, and was intended as a pilot for a series that never happened. An assigned task, with a script that even after it had been intensively reworked was still uninspiring, it did little to push Spielberg's career and was very quickly buried.

4. Two Losers

At last a feature-film idea was reaching the point at which it could be turned into reality. The screenwriters Hal Barwood and Matthew Robbins had worked over the story Spielberg had considered earlier, that of the Texas couple kidnapping a policeman in an attempt to gain access to their children. They had been encouraged by the veteran producer Jennings Lang, who had taken an interest in Spielberg. Then in a bout of Hollywood politics Lang was eased out and Richard Zanuck and David Brown took over the project, intending to make the film at Universal, the studio that had earlier put it in turnaround, that chilling filmland word denoting a lack of interest, when Lew Wasserman, the president of the company, had declared that the story of two losers would have no general appeal. Zanuck and Brown were a hot production team and allowed Spielberg plenty of artistic freedom, which was a remarkable mark of confidence in view of the fact that this was his first pure theatrical film.

The storyline of the new work, now called *The Sugarland Express* after the town that is the destination for the protracted chase, was changed considerably in order to make the mother the more important of the two main characters. It was she who was to be the instigator of the plot, and the organizer of the escape of her convicted husband during a visiting period at the pre-release centre where he is finishing his sentence. It was she who was to be the catalyst for the seizure of the state trooper and his vehicle, and eventually the cause of her weak spouse's doom as a consequence of her insistent desire that he should drive up to the house to claim the children, when common sense would suggest that almost certainly an official ambush would be waiting for him. The main part of the film is concerned with the cross-country chase, with a convoy of dozens of squad cars following the couple's progress, and their elevation to fifteen-minute media fame, as the television coverage prompts the entire population of the small towns through which the bizarre procession passes to turn out and wave them through as popular folk heroes.

The casting of the semi-literate Lou Jean Poplin was challenging. The woman was strong-willed and impetuous, but not very bright, and so a danger to those around her. Yet she had to evoke sympathy for her need to pursue her maternal instincts to the exclusion of everything else. Spielberg lit on Goldie Hawn, then still mainly thought of as the dizzy blonde in *Rowan and Martin's Laugh In* on television. She had won an Oscar for her supporting role in *Cactus Flower*, but had never before attempted a serious dramatic part. Her limp husband Clovis was played by William Atherton, who adroitly basked in her shadows, and the unfortunate policeman was Michael Sacks. Ben Johnson took the role of the senior police officer in charge of the operation to liberate the officer, and whose intention not to resort to violence is betrayed.

Hawn had a difficult time suppressing her bubbling natural talent for comedy, but Spielberg patiently brought her performance down, and can be said to have turned her into a versatile actress. Her presence had been a helpful factor in the financing, and her portrayal duly met his criteria.

Shot on country roads in Texas around San Antonio, *The Sugarland Express* demonstrates Spielberg's early mastery of complicated logistics. Even with his massive cavalcade of police cars he was able to marshal them in ever-interesting formations, and to create striking visuals, ensuring that the skills of his cinematographer Vilmos Szigmond were constantly stretched. The multi-car police chase was to become a cliché when other directors copied it. Spielberg's confident style belied the fact that this was his first full-blown theatrical film, and it was favourably received by the critics, who recognized that a spectacular new directing talent had emerged. Yet it was poorly accepted by the public. In some respects the presence of Hawn was off-putting, leaving audiences unprepared for the ultimate tragedy. In fact, a happy ending was never an option. Spielberg liked to compare his film with Billy Wilder's scathing attack on the manipulation of public hysteria, *Ace in the Hole*. In more ways than one it is an apt parallel, since Wilder's film, in spite of its merit, was also a box-office failure. It seemed that the shrewd old Wasserman had guessed right after all. The public was not interested in the two losers.

5 Shark Behaving Badly

Almost every year there is one film that receives more media attention than any other, and word-of-mouth requires it to be seen by anybody who wants to stay in the social swim. Producers marvel at its grosses, the public clamour to go to it, the theatre owners accept special conditions, and for weeks it is a talking point, inspiring newspaper cartoons, comedians' wisecracks and critics' in-depth analyses. In 1975 that film was *Jaws*. The story of the hunt for a great white shark that causes havoc in a small east-coast beach resort, by attacking and killing swimmers with sudden, ruthless ferocity, caught the public imagination to a degree that bordered on the hysterical, and caused considerable paranoia in real seaside communities, where bathers became reluctant to take to the sea, fearful that reality should imitate art. It was the first film to take $100 million at the box office, and eventually reached a worldwide total of more than $500 million. It is one of the biggest earners in the history of film, and with adjustments for inflation is still ranked among the top five.

The source was a melodramatic adventure novel by Peter Benchley which had been a best-seller, but even before its publication Zanuck and Brown had bought it for $175,000, giving the author more for writing the screenplay, and also a percentage of takings. Their preferred director was Dick Richards, a seasoned, if uninspiring hand. Spielberg read the proof copy on Brown's desk and found that something in the story was exerting a neurotic effect on him, possibly because he had moved house from Laurel Canyon to Malibu, and had taken to staring out to sea. His request to direct it was rejected, but a few days later Richards withdrew, so Zanuck and Brown approached Spielberg, who had meanwhile decided that he did not want to do it after all. To persuade him the producers agreed to several important conditions, including the discarding of Benchley's sub-plot, most of which consisted of a love story which Spielberg saw as a maritime *Peyton Place* soap opera. He wanted to build the film around the shark, even though the creature would not actually be seen until more than an hour of running time had elapsed. The great white, however, would have established an invisible presence within the opening minutes, and the grisly results of its attacks would generate an inescapable atmosphere of menace, charging the action accordingly. Because Benchley's early drafts were almost literal reinterpretations of the book, Spielberg brought in other writers, including Howard Sackler and Carl Gottlieb, who shared the eventual screen credit. An inserted dialogue passage recalling the gruesome wartime sinking of USS *Indianapolis*, with many of its drowning crew eaten by sharks, was written by John Milius.

The chosen location for the story, which Gottlieb described as '*Moby Dick* meets *Enemy of the People*', was Martha's Vineyard, an island off the south coast of Massachusetts where there were miles of sandy beaches and dunes. The small port of Edgarstown was chosen to represent the fictitious town of Amity. Three mechanical sharks that would be interlinked with general shots of live sharks were constructed at Universal, but in the salty Atlantic waters they malfunctioned, causing distress during production, sometimes even sinking straight to the bottom. Spielberg was under intense strain during most of the shooting, while the overrun on the schedule mounted, and privately he despaired, aware that with his first film a box-office failure, and *Jaws* moving along so slowly and costing a fortune in delays, his reputation back in Hollywood was likely to sink with the shark. The misbehaving mechanicals were only a part of many problems. Other mishaps included the loss of a couple of cameras and a few potentially serious accidents involving both cast and crew members. Press interest was intense, and the jinxed production acquired the nickname 'Flaws'. Word got around that the shark was a phoney, and a certain amount of bad-mouthing followed. Delays occurred during shooting because sightseers' boats entered the camera eyeline, enraging Spielberg, who wanted the sea clear to the horizon.

There are three main humans in *Jaws*. The first is the local police chief, played by Roy Scheider, a landlubber obliged to turn into action man afloat in order to protect his community and the livelihood of its traders after their summer turns sour with shark hysteria driving the visitors away. He is placed under tremendous pressure when the mayor (Murray Hamilton) assumes that a small shark that has been washed up dead is the villain of the piece, an illusion shattered by an ichthyologist played by Richard Dreyfuss, the second leading character. He is a scientist with a special passion for great whites, which in one blood-chilling phrase he describes as created by nature for nothing other than killing, 'a perfect engine – an eating machine'. The last of the main characters is a rugged, scarred bounty hunter of the ocean, played by the British actor Robert Shaw, who becomes profoundly obsessed, like Captain Ahab in *Moby Dick*, with finding and destroying the monster, which eventually claims him. Spielberg modified Benchley's original visualization of his death, a noble Melville-style end in which he is swept into the depths by his marine nemesis, and instead made it repulsive, sudden and shocking, one of the moments of terror that brought audiences to the edges of their seats. The three of them set out in Shaw's small, vulnerable fishing boat to track the twenty-eight-foot-long predator, but in so doing anger it to the point that it attacks and upturns their vessel in a terrifying climactic scene.

The most celebrated terror effect comes right at the beginning, a much-parodied sequence, in which a young woman skinny-dips by moonlight, with John Williams's insistent, pounding theme music making it clear that something very nasty is about to happen to her. Spielberg had no need to reveal the shark at this point. The sudden foamy eruption of the water around her and the subsequent swirl of blood are quite enough.

Spielberg used other camera shocks with remarkable assurance. In one shot Scheider is tossing bloody swill into the water and turns his head to talk to Dreyfuss and Shaw, who are otherwise engaged. The audience sees even before he does the enormous head of the shark, seeming to consist mostly of teeth, rearing out of the water. Startled, Scheider retreats, his cigarette still stuck to his lips. The others have not seen it. He says to Shaw, who is in the wheelhouse, 'We're going to need a bigger boat.' It is the dramatic entrance of the leading performer, halfway through the 124-minute film.

In spite of its then unprecedented commercial success, which followed an unparalleled level of publicity and advertising (the budget for the latter was nearly $2 million, a record sum), Spielberg was personally disappointed that after the arduous five-and-a-half-month shoot the film did not turn out as he would have hoped. Many sequences involving the shark were dropped because of the technical problems. In order to gain a PG rating, which would allow the film to play to a family audience, some of the grisliest scenes were cut from the final edit. Although he had excised much of Benchley's domestic trivia, most of the onshore scenes involving Scheider's home life were banal, and dissipated the tension of the central drama. A scene, shot in a Beverly Hills swimming pool, was also added to allow a half-eaten corpse to bob out of a sunken boat and give Richard Dreyfuss and most of the audience a monumental fright. Peter Benchley, who was given a cameo role as a television journalist, was publicly scornful of Spielberg's changed emphasis.

In fact, in many respects the film is closer to *Duel* than it is to later Spielberg films, in that there is no sentimentality: it is simply the story of puny ones taking on a mighty predator. The input of the editor, Verna Fields, was crucial in maintaining the excitement, but Spielberg somehow managed to preserve a light touch, and in spite of the chilling nature of the horror sequences there is plenty of wry humour.

The Academy spurned Spielberg, and although *Jaws* was nominated for best picture, the Oscar in that year was won by *One Who Flew Over*

During the shooting of Jaws **Spielberg privately despaired as the film overran on schedule and budget. He felt his reputation back in Hollywood was likely to sink with the shark.**

the Cuckoo's Nest. Milos Forman, its director, also picked up the direction award, for which Spielberg was not even nominated. It would not be the last time that his success would go unrecognized by the old Hollywood establishment. Another consequence of *Jaws* was the advent of a veritable avalanche of inferior rip-offs, not counting its own sequels, none of which came near to matching the fresh impact of the original, in which communities were menaced by killer whales, killer bears, killer ants, even killer bees. The other effect was to reinvent the blockbuster, the kind of film that was hyped-up to appear so big that special distribution arrangements had to be made, involving heavier commitments from exhibitors and even higher seat prices. The number of prints struck was multiplied so that the film could open in thousands of cinemas simultaneously. The old leisurely release pattern in which it would take many weeks, if not months, for a film to trickle through the cinemas came to an end as producers realized that audiences responded best when the publicity was running at its maximum power, more than compensating for the added expense of creating extra prints.

6 'Watch the Skies'

After *Jaws* Spielberg was in the most favourable position that a young director still in his twenties could expect to be. In a town where personal ratings are only as good as the last picture, his name was now widely known to the public, and he was even treated with respect by critics. Most importantly he had become elevated to the position of the foremost bankable director in Hollywood, an enviable niche to fill, giving him, in spite of the Academy's aloofness, the freedom to develop material without the usual suited phalanx of nay-sayers to thwart him. He was also about to meet, through his friend Brian De Palma, a young New York actress from a theatrical background who, although Jewish, had been raised as a Christian Scientist. Amy Irving was soon living with him, and they moved into a large new home in Coldwater Canyon in Beverly Hills. They would not marry until 1985, after the birth of their son Max.

Directors of Spielberg's creativity rarely begin each new project afresh. While they are working on one, another is simmering. Sometimes the process can last for years as an idea in development is elbowed aside to allow for one that has reached a more advanced stage to go into production. The next film in the Spielberg canon had been bubbling away for a considerable time, ever since his teenage years in fact. The project that he had been anxious to turn into a film had gone through several stages, but had been rejected in a number of places because the treatment of the subject matter was not considered to be good box office. The theme of UFOs had long fascinated him, having spent most of his childhood in Arizona, a state that has a much higher record of sightings than most others. It is perhaps significant that UFO landings, alien abductions and similar phenomena always occur in sparsely populated regions where there is not much else for the inhabitants to do other than cruise the highways in pick-up trucks looking for the next roadside bar. It seems perhaps inconsistent of them that UFOs never land in Massachusetts, and aliens, in order to further their understanding of human wisdom, never apparently kidnap Harvard professors. The presence in the open spaces of the southwest of covert military installations, and the testing of aircraft on secret lists, have certainly helped the mythology of extraterrestrial visitations along, although not all of the reports of UFO activity can be explained satisfactorily. The desert is a strange place to be in at night under a clear sky. There appears to be so much of it, with each star finely etched in the glowing canopy. It is not hard to find a mood to conjure up thoughts of extraterrestrial travel. Spielberg, like millions of other Americans, including President Carter, is a believer in something out there.

Shortly after the Spielbergs had moved to the Phoenix area, his father had taken him out into the desert in the middle of the night to join hundreds of others who had driven there in order to watch a dazzling light display in the heavens. It was a natural phenomenon, a meteor shower, but far away from city streetlights it could be seen as a dazzling spectacle, and he was impressed by the awed spirit of the watching crowd. 'Watch the skies' became a motto for him, and was the title of the first UFO film that he planned to make after he had become a full-time professional movie-maker. It would have been a souped-up remake of his teenage film *Firelight*.

Although he grew up on the alien-invasion films of the fifties, led by *War of the Worlds*, *The Thing* and *Invasion of the Body Snatchers*, in which malevolent creatures from elsewhere attempted to conquer Planet Earth by destructive force, Spielberg wanted to suggest that his visitors came with benign intentions. Initially a screenplay had been written by Paul Schrader, but he found it unworkable, and resolved now to start again, writing it afresh himself. It went through six drafts, and he also had input from a number of other screenwriters, including Hal Barwood and Matthew Robbins, although the director took the sole screenplay credit. He was keen to establish it as 'a Steven Spielberg film', a form of billing that has become commonplace to the point of boredom, and with the help of his producers, Julia and Michael Phillips, who felt that his claim was justified, he succeeded.

The new film, now called *Close Encounters of the Third Kind* – the first is the sighting of a UFO, the second is physical evidence of it, and the third is physical contact – was conceived to be on an epic scale, and was made by the financially stretched Columbia Pictures with an initial budget of $16 million, although the final figure was more than $22 million. During the post-production period the studio head, David Begelman, was spectacularly caught with his hand in the till, provoking a Hollywood scandal that still causes shudders throughout the industry, and Spielberg's film carried the unhealthy onus of the company's survival on its shoulders, a difficult task in view of the unhealthily high budget, which called for a huge return at the box office if it was to go into profit.

Production began in May 1976, after exhaustive pre-production work which entailed extensive travel across the western United States looking for locations, particularly the peculiarly shaped mountain that was to

serve as a beacon for the incoming mother ship. The team settled on
Devil's Tower, Wyoming, not because it was particularly high, but
because its truncated shape, like a cone with the point sliced off leaving
a flat top, was distinctive enough to make an instantly recognizable
image. The set Spielberg needed for his landing site would have been far
too big to fit on to a Hollywood sound stage, and was constructed in an
enormous hangar, originally built to accommodate military dirigibles, in
Mobile, Alabama. It had size, being larger than a football pitch and six
times bigger than the biggest sound stage in Hollywood, but lighting it
was a costly nightmare, and there were so many production hold-ups that
Spielberg compared his hangar with the mechanical shark in *Jaws*.

There was also a sequence shot in India where an enormous crowd
points to the sky in order to show where their encounter of the first kind
had taken place. The veteran British cinematographer Douglas Slocombe
was engaged to shoot it, although the cinematographer for the rest of the
film was Vilmos Szigmond.

The leading actor was played by Richard Dreyfuss, the ocean scientist in *Jaws*, who came to it after Jack Nicholson, Al Pacino and Gene
Hackman had been considered but were for various reasons unable to
take it on. Spielberg had all along regarded the special effects as the true
stars of the film, but Dreyfuss proved to be an admirable choice to play
an ordinary man who is chosen by the aliens as their conduit to communication with mankind. He takes the role of an electricity lineman in
Muncie, Indiana, and in the course of investigating a rural blackout
encounters an enormous UFO on the highway. It immobilizes his truck
and fills the night sky with a dazzling light. The experience changes his
life, threatening his marriage (Teri Garr plays his wife) and his sanity,
when his home is besieged by UFOs. He destroys his kitchen to build a
model of a mountain that seems to exist inside his head, but when he
realizes after it is finished that it is Devil's Tower he resolves to reach it.
Meanwhile, on an official level the phenomena are being investigated. A
squadron of wartime fighter planes suddenly materializes in the desert,
in exactly the same condition in which they vanished in the forties when
they entered the Bermuda triangle and never emerged. With a French
scientist (François Truffaut) abetting the government, attempts are
mounted to make contact with the aliens who let it be known that Devil's
Tower is their preferred conference site. Dreyfuss and a woman (Melinda
Dillon) he had met at the first close encounter, and whose small boy
(Cary Guffey) has been abducted by the aliens, having journeyed to
Wyoming, find that the entire area around Devil's Tower has been
cordoned off. They manage, after they have been ordered away, to break
into it and at night climb through the brush to the summit, there to
discover the landing site. What follows is the most amazing spectacle

that man can have witnessed as small space ships stage a kind of extraterrestrial air display, leading to the arrival of the gigantic mother ship, ablaze with light like an airborne Las Vegas. After making its greetings with variations on a five-note musical theme, echoed by flashing lights which are interpreted by the Earth scientists' computers, a dialogue ensues and eventually the portals of the ship open and aliens emerge, followed by humans who have been thought of as lost or dead, including Dillon's four-year-old small son. In the final moments some earthling volunteers, Dreyfuss included, choose to depart in the mother ship, on a voyage of understanding. It was a deeply troubled production. The astonishing final sequence of *Close Encounters of the Third Kind* absorbed more than half of the shooting schedule, and the nervous tension at Columbia back in Los Angeles increased daily as the costs mounted. Producer Julia Phillips developed severe antipathy towards the director of photography, Vilmos Szigmond, and tried to have him replaced with a faster cinematographer. She herself was in the throes of severe cocaine dependancy, which she has described in her book *You'll Never Eat Lunch in This Town Again*, and her inconsistent behaviour and unfortunate comments to the media produced a negative effect that eventually led to her dismissal by David Begelman in the post-production stage. She had also objected to the casting of the European director and Spielberg's idol, François Truffaut, as the French scientist, although his performance was attractive and apt, displaying an eagerness and enthusiasm that were entirely characteristic of his own persona, and was one of the surprising elements in the film. Spielberg, awed by Truffaut's towering reputation and his own shared cineaste's appreciation of Hitchcock and Lean, was flattered to find that the Frenchman also admired him, particularly for the skill with which he could take on probably the most formidable logistical burden that had ever befallen an American director. To the credit of both film-makers, neither was intimidated by the presence of the other, and Truffaut did not attempt to tell Spielberg how to do it, while Spielberg was happy to allow Truffaut to enact his performance entirely naturally, with a minimum of help.

Truffaut found the interminable shooting period burdensome, and was itching to leave to make his next movie. He was heard to remark, on learning that one shot had cost $250,000, that he could have made an entire film on such a budget. Later, in a *New York Times* interview Truffaut directed his venom at Julia Phillips, blaming her for the production confusions and describing her as incompetent. In her book she says, uncharmingly, of him: 'Of all the dead people I know he wins the prick award hands down.'

The special effects added another $3.2 million to the budget, and were in the charge of Douglas Trumbull, who had supervised Stanley

Kubrick's *2001: A Space Odyssey*. His work on *Close Encounters* was so complex and mysterious that the actors often had very little idea what was actually meant to happen or what they were supposed to be looking at. Techniques that have now become commonplace were pioneered, particularly computer-generated imagery (CGI), which was then in its infancy. A system was devised to synchronize the camera movements on miniatures with their full-size counterpart. When the small UFOs tear along state highways, for instance, and streak at speed through a toll station to the bemusement of its staff, their lights are exactly matched as reflections in the booth windows. The effects were planned in detail months in advance and set lighting was carried out to allow for the addition of other constituents at a later date. The biggest challenge was the creation of the mother ship, the airborne behemoth that fills the sky as it comes into land. Its appearance was said to have been inspired by a nocturnal view of an oil refinery, with hundreds of tiny lights illuminating complex industrial mechanisms. When finally it opens up its interior seems filled with dazzling light through which the aliens, played by little girls in huge full-head masks and sheer skintight catsuits, slowly appear, the lighting so bright as though the film stock has been greatly overexposed that they take on an ethereal, other-world quality.

The final element that was to make a significant artistic contribution was the score. John Williams, the composer of the *Jaws* theme, had to overcome several challenges, including the composition of the five-note alien communicating theme (later borrowed as a door chime in the James Bond film *Moonraker*) and to incorporate at the least the spirit if not the actual notes of 'When You Wish Upon a Star' from Disney's *Pinocchio*, which Spielberg saw as an inspiration for what his film was about (Teri Garr applies a Pinocchio name, Jiminy Cricket, to her husband after he has been consumed by his obsession). Originally the song was to have ended the film, but preview audiences did not take well to it, and Williams's own closing theme was substituted.

Spielberg had maintained a closed set, and conducted the editing and other post-production in secret. His late tinkerings delayed the release and upset the publicity schedule. A journalist working for *New York* magazine inveigled his way with a $25 bribe into a sneak preview in Dallas, and, although advance reviews had been embargoed, wrote a negative piece. He was not a film critic but a personal finance writer, and his view was that Spielberg's film did not measure up to the current box-office leader, George Lucas's *Star Wars*, and moreover, it would be a terrible flop. The beleaguered shareholders in Columbia, who had seen the stock gradually rise from $7 to $18 in anticipation that Spielberg's film would save the studio, took another beating when it plunged back sharply on the strength of the adverse article, and so concerted was the

rush to unload the shares that the New York Stock Exchange temporarily suspended trading in them. *Time* magazine, friendly by virtue of
investment, ran a positive piece by critic Frank Rich, who argued that its
originality and daring approach would ensure that it was a box-office hit.
The slide was halted. The film opened to glowing reviews and an even
more enthusiastic response from the public. It was chosen for the annual
Royal Film Performance in London, and Spielberg attended to meet the
Queen with other members of the cast and production executives.
Neither Julia Phillips nor David Begelman were present. Spielberg's film
was eventually to gross $240 million worldwide, making it one of the
biggest successes of all time. He had achieved the extraordinary feat of
having managed to direct two megahits one after the other.

Much of the popular appeal of *Close Encounters* resided in the way that
Spielberg had taken such an extraordinary event as a mass incursion of
spacecraft from elsewhere, placed it in a mundane, instantly familiar
Middle American setting, in this case Muncie, Indiana, and shown the
reactions of sceptical ordinary people, halfway ready to believe in
government conspiracies and cover-ups. The Richard Dreyfuss character is a blue-collar Everyman, and that he should be chosen to serve as
a sort of Earth ambassador on the visitors' mother ship is a bold populist
gesture. Spielberg's fascination for unexplained phenomena can be
sneered at on a higher intellectual level as naive and unscientific, placing him on the same level as the readers of the *National Inquirer* and
other supermarket tabloids that exploit the tastes of gullible readers for
the incredible. Yet in the way he uses it in his films he is also satisfying
an innate yearning in people for the fulfilment of fantasies. The uncriti-
cal mind hungers for knowledge of worlds beyond our own, as if there
lies somewhere out there an explanation for mankind's irrationality and
unease. In some ways a belief in the phenomena of UFOs performs a
similar function to religion, without the baggage of guilt that most faiths
insist on imposing. Spielberg's sense of wonder at the miracles of the
universe may have a childlike dimension, but therein lies the universally
seductive appeal of his approach. His film opens adult eyes to the infinity of possibility that many children but few adults are able to perceive.
This philosophy would reach its apogee with the realization of *ET The
Extra-Terrestrial*. It is the side of him that never grew up, and gave him
the uniqueness that qualified him to become the most popular film-
maker in the history of cinema.

Psychologists might be tempted to argue that Spielberg exhibited
another recognizable childish trait, that of anal retention, a resistance to
letting a project go. Setting a bizarre precedent, two years after the
release of *Close Encounters of the Third Kind* he started shooting new
scenes, and embarked on a re-editing of the entire film. The so-called

Special Edition, his second thoughts, was slightly shorter than the original in spite of new footage, as Spielberg had trimmed large chunks of the central section, including the manic behaviour of Dreyfuss as he builds his model of Devil's Tower from garbage and scraps in his kitchen. Added were scenes of a cargo ship that had been lost in the Bermuda triangle, turning up in the Gobi desert, and a scene in which Dreyfuss, seriously disturbed, is found cowering in the shower. The most significant addition was an end sequence showing what Dreyfuss found when he went on board the mother ship, which Spielberg later claimed had been insisted upon by the studio as a *quid pro quo* in allowing him a budget for such an extraordinary indulgence. His instinct was correct for inevitably the interior, a kind of translucent, glowing, dreamlike atrium lobby, is an anticlimax. The new version was seen in some quarters as an improvement on the original, since the story developed rather faster, but purists were disappointed by what they felt was unnecessary tinkering and much preferred it as they had first seen it. Unlike Disney's forthcoming amended version of *Fantasia*, which involved the suppression of the 1940 film, both editions were intended to coexist, and Spielberg at a later date professed an admiration for the original. It seems that Columbia, in allowing him to engage in his strange fancy, were only attempting to cream even more profits from a highly commercial work.

7 Comedy or Disaster?

Spielberg's Hollywood clout, apart from the ability to win Oscars, which still eluded him, increased even further with the *Close Encounters* success. But there was to follow a painful experience when his judgement, normally so sensitive to the public appetite, deserted him for what was to be the most expensive fiasco of his career. He had backed a couple of young film-makers, Robert Zemeckis and Bob Gale, whose student work had impressed him, to make a film based on Beatlemania and New Jersey teenagers anxious to see their idols perform in New York on their first American trip, which culminated in an appearance on the Ed Sullivan Show. Their film, *I Wanna Hold Your Hand*, written by both of them and directed by Zemeckis, featured a cast of unknowns apart from Nancy Allen, who was married to Brian De Palma. It had a great deal of charm and humour, and the atmosphere of 1964 was accurately rendered. It was also a resounding flop, and even Spielberg's credit as executive producer could not induce the young of 1978 to take an interest in what their parents had been up to fourteen years earlier.

Zemeckis and Gale had also written, at the behest of John Milius, a script called *The Night the Japs Attacked*, the gung-ho offensiveness of the title reflecting the right-wing leanings of the writer-director, an acknowledged gun freak. Spielberg and Milius frequently met socially, and the idea developed that Spielberg would turn it into a film. The historic basis of *1941*, as the film of the script was called, was a very minor incident in World War II when an offshore Japanese submarine fired at some oil wells near Santa Barbara. Although the attack was small beer in comparison with what was happening in other theatres of war, it was the first time that an enemy power had assailed the mainland of the United States since the war of 1812, and given the extent of post-Pearl Harbor paranoia, Los Angeles was put on full alert, with anti-aircraft guns popping off at unidentified targets, while rumours that the Japanese were mounting a gigantic aerial blitz, and that massed formations of heavy bombers were flying in for the kill, were rampant. A panic ensued, which was very quickly forgotten when the degree of the false alarm

1941 began with a parody of Jaws: the naked girl is surprised, not by a shark, but by a surfacing submarine that hoists her aloft on its periscope.

became realized, leaving many people as red-faced as those easterners who in 1938 had believed that the Orson Welles radio version of *The War of the Worlds* was real, and had taken to the hills in fright.

Spielberg wanted to build the episode into an elaborate farce, which was hardly his metier, and made the miscalculation of attempting to film it as a blockbusting epic, on an appropriate budget, with elaborate special effects and gigantic sets, as well as many explosions and destructive collapses. He had become affected by the anarchic humour of John Belushi, a regular performer on the NBC comedy show *Saturday Night Live*, who had more or less single-handedly made the inane and anarchic *National Lampoon's Animal House*, directed by John Landis, into a substantial hit. Initially Spielberg had considered him for the role of the Japanese submarine commander, but as further ideas developed he decided instead to make him a chaotic, crazy, cigar-chomping pilot of a P–40 combat aircraft who, after landing at a roadside gas station in Death Valley, imagines that he is taking on squadrons of Zeros, and in going after them devastates half of Hollywood. The submarine was now to be commanded by the distinguished Japanese actor Toshiro Mifune, with Christopher Lee playing a high-ranking Nazi naval officer on board as an observer. Continuing the impressive casting, Robert Stack was put in the role of General 'Vinegar Joe' Stilwell, who at the time of Pearl Harbor was in charge of Californian coastal defence. As the crisis outside develops he is sitting in a movie theatre watching his favourite sentimental film, Walt Disney's delightful animated feature about an elephant, *Dumbo*. Meanwhile Tim Matheson, a USAAF captain, is making a play for the general's secretary Nancy Allen, who is sexually stimulated by aircraft; Bobby De Cicco, having exchanged his zoot suit for a sailor's uniform, is taking part in an energetic USO jitterbug contest; and the enemy submarine commander is preparing a strike against Hollywood, the seat of western decadence, for the honour of the Imperial Japanese Navy. Belushi's SNL colleague, Dan Aykroyd, also had a telling part as a blinkered, trigger-happy tank sergeant who starts firing wildly with his cannon. Ned Beatty plays a householder on the coast who engages the submarine offshore at Santa Monica with the gun that the army has parked in his backyard, and whose house is wrecked in retaliation.

Spielberg chose to begin his film with a parody of the opening sequence of *Jaws* – with a girl (the same actress, Susan Backlinie, was hired again) swimming nude in the moonlight as the ominous throbbing of the musical theme is heard on the soundtrack. Instead of being devoured by a shark she is surprised by a surfacing submarine, and is hoisted aloft on the periscope. It was just one of Spielberg's miscalculations. It was all right for *Saturday Night Live* to mock his films, and its *Jaws* parody had become renowned, but it was considered somewhat self-regarding for a director to make such a deliberate reference to his own work.

Notwithstanding the research budget for period detail, historical verisimilitude was abandoned. The Santa Barbara incident of February 1942 was brought forward to December 1941 and the first week of America's entry into the war. To add further confusion to the muddled situation, somehow the zoot-suit riots are roped in, although they did not occur until two years later, and no attempt is made to explain their real origin in interracial conflicts, with the result that the reference was seen as an insensitive exploitation of black heritage. Spielberg, following the lead from Milius, was at pains not to make the film politically correct in any way, regarding its flippant approach to the serious subject of war hysteria as being in the vein of earlier comedies that had pushed back the barriers of good taste with casual abandon. But where Lubitsch in *To Be Or Not To Be*, Preston Sturges in *Hail the Conquering Hero*, and even Stanley Kubrick and his *Dr Strangelove* had evoked the power of satire to wring laughter from the most cataclysmic circumstances, Spielberg was reducing it all to destructive farce. He seemed so carried away with the spectacle of catastrophe that it was almost as if he was really directing a disaster movie. The big Ferris wheel at Santa Monica breaks loose and runs away into the Pacific, rolling along the pier like an illuminated hoop before it topples off the end to sink beneath the waves. Belushi's P–40, after engaging the aircraft that Matheson and Allen have illicitly commandeered in order to make love in flight, and chasing it up and down Hollywood Boulevard, which resembles the clefts through which the X-fighters race in *Star Wars*, shoots them down in the La Brea Tar Pits, then itself crashes in a crumpled heap in the middle of the street, with the pilot baling out although he is only two feet from the ground. As a final touch for the end credits, Ned Beatty's semi-destroyed house slides off its clifftop, leaving behind a scene of total devastation looked on in amazement by almost the entire cast.

Spielberg likened his comedy to Norman Jewison's often overlooked 1966 film *The Russians Are Coming! The Russians Are Coming!* in which a Soviet submarine inadvertently invades a small island off New England. It was made on a fraction of the budget of *1941*. A much closer parallel to the inflated Spielberg production is the frenetic Stanley Kramer comedy of 1963, *It's a Mad Mad Mad Mad World*, which boasted a formidable array of stars and ends in a climactic orgy of destruction that leaves most members of the cast in hospital. Kramer, like Spielberg, learned very painfully that if large sums of money were hurled at the screen it did not make comedy funnier. The primary publishing spin-off connected with *1941* seems to have been a comic book from Heavy Metal/Arrow which in the graphic style of the medium echoes the film's visuals. But its format also helps to explain the mindless characterization which makes so much of the motivation impossible to discern. Spielberg's own self-deluding introduction to the comic book says at one

Spielberg was so carried away with the spectacle in 1941
it was almost as if he was directing a disaster movie.

point: 'I felt that after the war in Vietnam and the disillusionment the
nation experienced, it was important to remind people that war doesn't
have to be a trip up the river to hell; it could also be a lot of laughs.'

Yet contrary to the perception that still has general currency, *1941* was
not a box-office flop, and actually made a modest profit. Although it was
generally castigated by the critics, a few were able to find elements to
praise. Pauline Kael in the *New Yorker* called it 'an amazing orgiastic
comedy, with the pop culture of an era compacted into a day and a night'.
The jitterbug contest, for instance, before it degenerates into mindless
rioting, is exuberantly filmed by a technically proficient director. For
older filmgoers it was pleasing to see many familiar faces from earlier
days in character parts, including Elisha Cook Jr., Slim Pickens, Lionel
Stander and even the writer-director Sam Fuller. But the artistic failure
of his film to some extent was a case of hubris, a sharp reminder to
Spielberg of his fallibility, and a warning that however tempting it seems,
comedy is too difficult to be approached lightly.

8 The Archaeologist as Action Man

A chastened Spielberg approached his next project with greater wariness. The idea for *Raiders of the Lost Ark* had come from George Lucas three years earlier, and the film was to be a collaborative effort. Lucas, whose *Star Wars* had become the most profitable film of all time, stood on a level platform with Spielberg – between them they were the two most successful film-makers in Hollywood, and could drive an unprecedented production and distribution deal with their joint movie, which would require the studio to put up the negative cost interest-free. The pair would then take 60 per cent of the gross up to $100 million, after which it would be shared equally. Paramount accepted the terms after protracted negotiation. The decision was taken to make the film in England, at Elstree studios where *Star Wars* had been shot, as at that time there were financial advantages under United Kingdom tax laws, and an absence of the union problems that were bedevilling production in the United States. Douglas Slocombe was assigned as director of photography.

The screenplay, written by Lawrence Kasdan, attempted to recapture the adventure and atmosphere of the Saturday matinée serials that had enthralled an earlier generation of young filmgoers, with their absurd heroics, hair-raising chases and cliff-hanging instalment endings. The difference would lie in the production values, ensuring that the stars and thrills would fulfil the demands of a contemporary film audience not prepared to tolerate the cardboard scenery of the old days, or the lack of character motivation. No Saturday serial could ever boast so many thousands of extras, such exotic locations, such elaborately conceived special effects or such dazzling cinematography. The central figure is an archaeologist called Indiana Jones who, when not conducting class seminars on his Ivy League campus, is out in the field, a dashing action man in a wide-brimmed slouch hat and leather jacket, a bullwhip tucked in his belt, as he faces lunatic perils that suddenly elevate what hitherto had been thought of as a staid vocation into one of the most dangerous professions on earth. The part called for a rugged, outdoors hero with a sense of humour and a sneaking eye for the women. The first choice was Tom

Selleck, but after his television series, *Magnum PI*, proved to be a hit, he became unavailable. Harrison Ford, who was the next in line, was chosen. Ford had come to prominence playing Han Solo in *Star Wars*, but had been seen in small parts for some years. An attractive actor with a limited range, he nevertheless had sufficient presence to make the part work, and his performance was to define the role.

The film was to be in the form of a quest, and Philip Kaufman suggested that the object should be the Ark of the Covenant, the receptacle of the Ten Commandments. In Hebraic tradition it is a sacred lost artefact, possessing awesome mysterious power, and such a concept was more likely to appeal to the Jewish Spielberg than to the Methodist Lucas. By setting the film in the mid-thirties, when even a flight in a biplane was a heady adventure, the screenplay was able to incorporate a Nazi intervention in the search, using as its basis Hitler's known fascination for the occult. The globetrotting in *Raiders of the Lost Ark* is formidable, and the action flits easily from South American jungle to Tibet to Egypt. The pre-title sequence sets the mood for what is to follow although, as with the James Bond prologues, it has nothing to do with the rest of the film. Indiana Jones, or Indy, is exploring a booby-trapped cave in the jungle, looking for an object of desire. Most of the snares he manages to evade, but it looks as though he will have trouble with a gigantic stone ball that is bearing down on him at speed, and he runs to escape from it. As he breaks free and manages to sprint to his plane a horde of murderously angry natives are in pursuit. He takes off with no time to spare. Only when he is airborne does he discover that he is sharing the cockpit with a deadly snake. Although only a few minutes of running time have elapsed there has been enough exciting action for an entire film.

A split had occurred between Amy Irving and Spielberg, and she had moved to Santa Fe, New Mexico, a relaxed haven favoured by hippies and artists, which had a reputation in some Los Angeles circles as the place to go to find the inner self. As a consequence, she was not cast as the female lead. The part had actually been written with Debra Winger in mind, but eventually went to Karen Allen, who had been in *National Lampoon's Animal House*. She was unhappy about the way her character was written, and wanted to shed the demure aspects of the role. In the event she underwent an ordeal as arduous as that suffered by Tippi Hedren in Hitchcock's *The Birds*, except that in her case reptiles were the applied torture. For a snake-pit scene more than four thousand of the creatures were used, and she was obliged to wallow among them, with more being thrown on her head. The story went around that far fewer snakes were gathered back at the end of the shoot than had been present at the beginning, the rest having vanished into the dark recesses of the Elstree sound stage, ready to provide an unexpected hazard for the next production to be filmed there.

Later Allen unwisely criticized Spielberg in an interview, and her career was subsequently patchy. It was not so much that he had maliciously put it around that she was trouble, but that she had broken the unwritten rules of Hollywood, since *Raiders of the Lost Ark* eventually grossed more than $360 million worldwide, the biggest money earner that Paramount ever had until Robert Zemeckis made *Forrest Gump* in 1994. Lucas and Spielberg had also delivered their film within the allotted schedule and budget, and so were able to net considerable profits themselves under the deal that had originally been struck.

Because it was a collaborative work Spielberg had reigned in his creativity, and never regarded the film as having his personal signature like *Close Encounters of the Third Kind*. He and Lucas worked together harmoniously, and he was happy to make compromises that had he been solo would have been more difficult. A Nazi experimental aircraft, a 'flying wing', had been mocked up, and at a planning meeting when the cost of construction was revealed to be astronomical George Lucas broke the ends of the wings off the model, reducing it from four to two engines, and thus effecting a saving of a quarter of a million dollars. The most famous cost-cutting moment turned out to produce the best-remembered joke in the entire film. Harrison Ford, having fought his way around an Arab kasbah, suddenly comes face to face with a gigantic swordsman, who blocks his path and twirls his scimitar in a series of intricate passes as a prelude to engaging in combat. Ford simply pulls out his revolver and shoots him. Apparently the actor had been suffering from stomach runs contracted at the Tunisian location, and was anxious to finish the scene and retire to bed, so he had agreed with Spielberg on the serendipitous short cut. There was no corner-cutting where the stunt work was concerned. In one of the chases Indy uses his bullwhip to winch himself under a moving truck and then to board it. It looks impossibly difficult but the feat was performed for the camera. Ford used a stunt double on this occasion, but often tackled arduous physical feats himself, such as the escape from the rolling boulder in the opening sequence.

Star Wars had spawned an ancillary merchandizing industry in which the licensed manufacture of toys, dolls, colouring books and other artefacts yielded huge profits to Lucas without him having to do anything other than sign a few pieces of paper. Spielberg followed suit with *Raiders of the Lost Ark* – 10 per cent of the retail price of an *Indiana Jones* figure would go to the film-makers. The earnings from careful merchandizing can reach a figure on top of and equivalent to its box-office gross. It should be noted that the film's logo, with the title drawn in a style that was evocative of old pulp comics, was one of the cleverest marketing devices, to be copied *ad nauseam* for other films.

Raiders of the Lost Ark **was a collaborative effort by two of the most successful film-makers in Hollywood: Lucas and Spielberg.**

9 How To Be An Alien

The success of *Raiders of the Lost Ark* did not disguise Spielberg's apprehensions that the film represented rather less of his own work than his others. In some respects he felt like a journeyman on the set, working as a hired director in the tradition of the old studio age. Instinctively he felt that he needed to make a film that would be uniquely recognizable as his own. The result was to be his biggest money-spinner and one of the most successful films of all time. He returned to his 'Watch the Skies' theme, and visualised a story of a child meeting and achieving rapport with a creature from somewhere else in the universe. The alien would be lost and disorientated, feelings that a child, particularly from a one-parent family, would instantly recognize. It was a fantasy that Spielberg had nursed since his own childhood. During the making of *Raiders of the Lost Ark* he had confided his ideas to Melissa Mathison, the screenwriter girlfriend of Harrison Ford, and she came up with the storyline for the film that was to be *ET The Extra-Terrestrial*. Elliott, a ten-year-old boy living with his divorced mother, older brother and younger sister in California, finds hiding behind the house an alien creature, marooned by his colleagues, who have returned to their own planet. The lonely boy, empathizing with the extraterrestrial, protects him from human adults and hides him among his toys. The alien learns to speak English, largely by watching television, and becomes not only the child's playmate but a hit with his friends, and is smuggled around wrapped up in a blanket in a basket on the front of Elliott's bike. The grown-up world is portrayed as predatory, unfeeling and stupid, and it is left to Elliott and his schoolfriends to try to save ET from the scientists, who want to examine him as a biological specimen. He is ill and appears to be doomed, but the children stage a rescue, and ET's own kind reappears in their spaceship, having been summoned by a homemade radio.

Among ET's many gifts is the power of telekinesis, enabling the pursuers to be lost as the children soar into the air on their bicycles. The silhouetted image of Elliott riding with ET across the sky against a full moon was later adopted by Spielberg as a motif for his production company, Amblin Entertainment.

Central to the film's astonishing appeal was the physical appearance of the extraterrestrial, which was designed at a cost of $1.5 million by Carlo Rambaldi as an animatronic prop, although in longshot midget stunt men performed in an ET suit. There is nothing humanoid to be seen; it as if the concept of 'bug-eyed monsters' has been extended to make such creations cuddlesome. ET is small, less than four feet tall, bulbous-bellied, reptilian, wrinkled, a large head topping his stalk-like extendable neck. His wide mouth is capable of expression. His tiny up-tilted nose separates his huge, lidded eyes, shielded by massive brows. His limbs are scrawny with long, thin fingers, his chest can glow and reveal his heart beating. He is as grotesque as a gargoyle, but at the same time can exert a soulful, wistful appeal. Careful lighting also helped to convey the moods and humour of the character. In addition to telekinesis, ET was given special gifts of telepathy and advanced learning. At a significant moment he stretches out a bony digit to young Elliott, and in an image deliberately reminiscent of Michelangelo's Sistine Chapel ceiling and the depiction of the hand of God reaching out to Adam, power passes from one fingertip to the other.

For a Spielberg film the budget was relatively modest, a mere $10.5 million, including the cost of constructing the ET aninamatronics. He decided to dispense with his usual storyboard approach in which every shot was drawn in sequence, except for special effects scenes, and the direction is looser and more fluid than with his earlier films. The interior shooting took place in conditions of secrecy at the less prominent Laird International studios in Culver City, under the cover title *A Boy's Life*, the leaked impression being that it was a comedy about Californian adolescents. Spielberg has always been wary of set visitors, and tends not to allow journalists anywhere near him when he is filming. He has a memory of his early days at Universal, when he wandered from stage to stage, and ventured on to the set of Alfred Hitchcock's *Family Plot*. The portly director, who remains a Spielbergian idol, had him asked to leave without actually speaking to him himself. A more practical reason for Spielberg's apparently paranoid desire to keep the exact nature of his work secret is the fear that his ideas can be grabbed and used for a quick television 'spoiler' movie before he is able to finish his own work. He is not alone in taking such a view. Woody Allen prefers to keep even the titles of his work in progress under wraps as long as possible, and perhaps the most outstanding exemplar of directorial reticence is Stanley Kubrik, who requires everyone on the payroll to sign an unofficial equivalent of the Official Secrets Act.

There were problems that had to be sorted out over the genesis of ET. Another project, *Night Skies*, which he had intended to produce from a screenplay by John Sayles, was a science-fiction drama in which a dangerous band of extraterrestrials mounted an attack on a remote farm-house. Their leader is a creature who can kill by touching his victims with his bony finger. The only sympathetic member of the group befriends a child on the farm, and is left behind at the end. It is almost like the opening moments of *ET The Extra-Terrestrial*. Sayles, given the option of changing the concept for the film that Spielberg really wanted to make, passed it by on the grounds that he could not handle something so sweet and sentimental, so leaving the field clear for Mathison's screen-play. At the time nobody could forecast that the eventual film would be such a hit, and one of its surprising aspects is that Columbia, after study-ing market surveys, declined the project, with Frank Price, then in charge, allowing it to pass to Universal, a decision as lacking in foresight as that of the record producer who turned down the opportunity to sign the Beatles on the brink of their career.

Later there were accusations of plagiarism. The idea of marooned aliens in a hostile environment endeavouring to find a way home is not particularly original, and when it was seen how much revenue Spielberg's execution of the theme was generating there were several opportunists ready to claim, without success, that their concepts had been pilfered.

The casting of the boy to play Elliott was exhaustive, with more than 300 being interviewed. Finally the part went to Henry Thomas, who had appeared in a Sissy Spacek film, *Raggedy Man*. He had a solemn, controlled gravitas, unusual for a ten-year-old, and was able to make the empathizing scenes completely credible, as well as conveying dogged patience and the determination to save his friend, no matter what. His distracted mother was played by Dee Wallace and his sister by a scene-stealing Drew Barrymore, then aged seven. Elliott's elder brother was played by Robert MacNaughton, and a government official on the trail of ET who becomes sensitive to the situation, known as 'Keys', was played by Peter Coyote.

The film falls conventionally into three acts. The first section estab-lishes the wondrous nature of the situation, and embraces the mystery as the small boy attempts to lure the alien out of the hiding place with a trail of Reese's Pieces, one of the most successful instances of product place-ments ever. (Originally the confection was to have been M&Ms but nego-tiations with its parent company Mars were abortive as they felt the subject matter was unsuitable and frightening.) The second section is the lightest and the funniest, in which ET comes to terms with the workings of the average American home, and gets to know the television and the refrigerator, and moves on from sampling a Coca-Cola to consuming an entire six-pack of beer, which leads to extraterrestrial inebriation. The final sequence is the most menacing, as the authorities move in to appre-hend the visitor in the name of science and ET faces death from earthly

ET The Extra-Terrestrial **was a fantasy that Spielberg had nursed since his own childhood. It became one of the most popular family films of all time.**

pollution; and it is also the most uplifting, in that Elliott and his friends literally ride to the rescue, and the spaceship at the beginning returns to the woods to ferry ET back to his home, coupled with the surging orchestration of John Williams's theme. It is difficult for even the most hardened moviegoer not to feel the emotional pull. Spielberg had achieved the making of the most popular family film of all time.

It was not difficult to spot points of identification with Spielberg himself. He knew the isolation that resulted from a broken home, and the problems of making friends in a new setting. The middle-class suburban enclave of modern split-level homes was typical of much of western America, and was actually Northridge in the San Fernando Valley, but was not so very different from the housing developments around Scottsdale and Arcadia. The most poignant moment in the film comes at the end when Elliott, having achieved the almost impossible feat of reuniting ET with his own kind, has to say farewell, and resists the invitation to fly off with his friend. It is at that moment the little boy takes on his greatest responsibility by giving up his friend.

The unprecedented success of *ET The Extra-Terrestrial* led to a record gross of more than $700 million which, when adjusted for inflation, makes it the all-time record-breaker. It also generated huge revenues from the spin-off merchandise, Spielberg having now appreciated its importance. So assiduously did he attend to that area that in some quarters he was regarded as the biggest merchant of hype since Disney. Not all items for sale were official, and lawsuits had to be mounted to curb some of the more blatant rip-offs. The British release was delayed for several months, enabling the country to be flooded with pirate videotapes on such a scale that the distributors became alarmed that too many people would have already seen the film for it to be a hit when it did eventually reach the cinemas. At one time almost every London cab driver seemed to know how to get hold of a pirated tape as a special favour. Video piracy had become a growing menace with the advent of the domestic video cassette recorder. The notoriety of the *ET* case strengthened the industry's hand in devising effective ways of combatting the menace, and the British measures were singularly effective. At the beginning of the video revolution Spielberg had been opposed to releasing his films on that medium, but *ET* changed his views. From the video release he could expect to earn 50 per cent of the revenue, and given the size of the sales that sum came to $70 million. Once the VCR had become a standard item in almost every home the film industry made the pleasant discovery that even films that had flopped theatrically could still end up in profit.

10 The Down Side Comes Up

By bizarre coincidence Spielberg was engaged on another project at the time of the production of *ET*, which shared a similar suburban setting, but in comparison was like a bad dream. The sweetness of *ET* was replaced by dark malevolence. In *Poltergeist* a family discovers that a malignant evil presence is in their house and is out to destroy. Their home is not a spooky old house with a history, as in *The Amityville Horror* and many other Old Dark House movies, but a modern desirable residence with a double garage that has just been built alongside many others in a sparkling new development. The conduit to the supernatural entity is the little daughter (Heather O'Rourke) of attractive parents (Craig T. Nelson and JoBeth Williams) who is obsessed with the television, and claims to talk to people inside the set through the whirling static that fills the screen in the middle of the night when the regular stations are no longer transmitting. The ghost in the machine eventually kidnaps her, then an exorcist attempts to rescue her, and the house is filled with horror, while the swimming pool turns into a scene resembling a nightmare conception of judgement day as slimy corpses jostle to emerge in a protracted sequence of baroque horror. The villainous real estate developers, it would seem, have built over an old charnel pit without first removing the remains, and have thus unleashed the rage of the undead. Why something so medieval should exist in an area that looks like Scottsdale is not explained, but the intention is to provoke shocks without the expectation of too close an examination of the reason why.

The film escalates from mundane domesticity to the Grand Guignol chimera in phases culminating in a spectacular special-effects climax, in which the skills of George Lucas's Industrial Light & Magic company, which he had established near San Francisco, are given an amazing shop window to demonstrate their state-of-the-art proficiency.

The story of *Poltergeist* was Spielberg's own, and he supervised the production of the film and the final cut, to such an extent that he could almost have been its director. The directorial credit went to Tobe Hooper, the Texan responsible for the cult shocker *The Texas Chain-Saw Massacre*, a $350,000 exploitation film which had grossed $3 million and which Spielberg admired. For contractual reasons Spielberg was not able officially to direct *Poltergeist*, and his Universal contract kept him fully occupied with *ET*, but as the schedule was delayed he spent much time on Hooper's set, and quite clearly was doing everything that a director would normally do. Hooper was merely his mouthpiece, since Spielberg maintained a total proprietorial right over every aspect. The film was very successful at the box office, not least because in the advertising campaign Spielberg's name was billed twice as large as Hooper's. Also, under the Directors' Guild of America (DGA) rules, as producer he was not eligible for the directorial credit, and the organization upheld Hooper's case by having some offending trailers removed from theatres in the influential New York and Los Angeles release areas, while Spielberg issued a public apology to him in the form of an advertisement in the trade press. Yet it is fair to say that *Poltergeist* was in all but the finest detail a Spielberg film, and Hooper's own subsequent career was sadly lacklustre.

Trouble occurred on another Spielberg production. The old Rod Serling television series *The Twilight Zone* was being turned into a feature-length film, using four linked episodes, one of which was to be directed by Spielberg. Another was by his fellow enthusiast for the old television show, John Landis, the director of *National Lampoon's Animal House*, *An American Werewolf in London* and *The Blues Brothers*, and Spielberg was to be co-producer. In the Landis episode Vic Morrow was to play a racist who is transplanted to occupied France to feel what it was like to be persecuted by the Nazis as a Jew, then to the American south where he suffers lynch-law as a black at the hands of the Ku-Klux-Klan, and finally to Vietnam as a villager under fire from the American army. During the night filming of the Vietnam sequence some forty miles north of Los Angeles, a helicopter crashed, killing Morrow and two children who were playing Vietnamese children. Landis and two others were immediately charged with involuntary manslaughter, and during the investigation it was discovered that the strict rules on the hiring of minors for films had not been observed, that work permits had not been obtained and that the parents had not been warned that the scene was potentially dangerous. Given the charges, Landis, the director, faced a prison sentence, and Spielberg was the co-producer.

There were inevitable rumours that Spielberg had been on the set on the fatal night, which was unlikely, and they were never proved. In fact Spielberg went to pains to distance himself from the whole affair and brought criticism on himself, while the well-oiled studio legal machine cracked into action to secure for Landis an eventual acquittal who, nevertheless, was reprimanded by the DGA for unprofessional conduct. There were also civil lawsuits brought by parents, but Spielberg was absolved. The deaths, however, troubled him greatly and although it was an accident it was clear that Landis's desire to get his shot in the can had taken precedence over everything else. Successful directors, like newspaper editors, often have a streak of ruthlessness that transcends normal standards of behaviour, and Landis had a hard reputation, putting him in the league of DeMille, Preminger and Peckinpah, who could also be monsters on the set. The affair did little for Hollywood's public image, which was already tarnished at the time after John Belushi's death from drug abuse on an operatic scale, together with various other well-publicized instances of cocaine and heroin dependency that had destroyed careers, not so much because the dependency caused moral outrage but from the sheer incapacity of the users to do their job properly. The Begelman embezzlement case was recapitulated in punishing detail in the book *Indecent Exposure* by David McClintick, and Francis Coppola's Zoetrope studios, with all its bright hopes dashed into oblivion, went spectacularly bankrupt.

The Landis episode of *Twilight Zone – The Movie* was, in spite of its tragic outcome, retained in the finished film. The second episode, directed by Spielberg, was set in an old folks' home to which Scarman Crothers comes and offers the inhabitants a one-off opportunity to experience what it is like to be young again, and after a taste of it they conclude that they are better off with their memories. Neither the Landis nor the Spielberg portions of the film are particularly effective. Spielberg's first inclination had been to abandon the production altogether, but Warner, whose film it was, felt that such a drastic step would be tantamount to an admission of guilt. So Spielberg proceeded but clearly without much enthusiasm. The third episode, directed by Joe Dante, in which a boy lures adults into a world created by his television-fed imagination and the fourth, with the Australian director of the *Mad Max* trilogy, George Miller, remaking one of the most celebrated of all *Twilight Zone* stories, 'Nightmare at 20,000 Feet' in which John Lithgow plays a nervous air passenger who notices during a bumpy flight that a hideous dwarf-like creature is hacking away at vital areas of the wing and engine, were adjudged to be far superior to the work of their better-known colleagues.

Even the phenomenal popularity of *ET The Extra Terrestrial* did not help Spielberg at the Academy Awards where, as had become the customary procedure, he was cold-shouldered in spite of nine nominations for the film. He was touched that Richard Attenborough, the director of *Gandhi*, which had swept up many of the major awards, generously consoled him and confided how deeply moved he had been by Spielberg's film.

It had been both the best and the worst year of his film-making career.

11 A Sidekick Called Short Round

The next feature that Spielberg would direct was a sequel to *Raiders of the Lost Ark*, which like its predecessor would be based at London's Elstree studios, and would also mark his return to his extensive story-boarding method. Entitled *Indiana Jones and the Temple of Doom*, it was to use some of the ideas that had been thought up for the first film, such as an impossible plunge from a crashing aircraft to safety on a life raft. Although the pulp-adventure yarn format was repeated, the tone had turned several shades darker in that Indy was now on the trail of an Asiatic villain, the leader of an evil sect who has snatched a precious jewel from a village, as well as abducting its children to make them work in his mines as chained slaves. Homage was paid to Hollywood's 1939 imperial adventure *Gunga Din*, which included incorporating an extraordinarily unfashionable element of racial xenophobia, and the Indian government, shocked by the script, refused permission for location work there, so Sri Lanka was used in lieu. Indiana Jones was given an assistant, a twelve-year-old urchin called Short Round (the young Vietnamese Ke Huy Quan) and a new heroine, Kate Capshaw, who played an American nightclub singer working in Shanghai who is swept along on the adventure. The action is supposed to take place a year or two earlier than *Raiders of the Lost Ark*, although Harrison Ford in the title role was visibly older. He was to suffer acute back pain from prolonged elephant riding. The opening sequence in which Capshaw renders, in Mandarin, Cole Porter's 'Anything Goes', a title chosen for its implicit message on the film's attitude, with a Hollywood-Chinese chorus attempting Busby Berkeley-style choreography, is the closest Spielberg has come to making a musical, and is staged with verve and excitement. Capshaw, as a ditsy, bubbly blonde, makes Karen Allen, the heroine of the first film, look sullen, butch and unamusing, and faces all her nightmare ordeals, such as an onslaught by thousands of crawling insects or suspension over a pit of molten lava, with comic-book screams, squirms and shrieks. The number at the beginning turns to chaos as frantic brawling, reminiscent of the jitterbug contest riot in *1941*, breaks out, and a precious gem slides across the floor to be muddled up and lost amid the spilt ice from a champagne bucket. The humour is often heavy-handed and uncomfortable, with the 'monkey brains' meal in which the most disgusting menu is served as a formal dinner that cannot be avoided a typical example.

The chases are brilliantly filmed, and in the mine-car sequence towards the end Spielberg's storyboarding produces a carefully worked-out progression of kinetic movement, with the energy and surprise of a theme-park ride, as though Spielberg was already thinking of a spin-off attraction for the Universal studio tour. It is a dazzling example of how Spielberg's care could produce the desired results, and looks far more dangerous than it actually was. Obviously, after the *Twilight Zone* tragedy Spielberg had elevated the safety of minors to primary importance.

As a further controversial aspect there was a considerable occult element, and some of its manifestations were disturbing, such as the passing of a hand through a body to seize and remove the beating heart from a victim of human sacrifice. The scene was trimmed for British distribution after one of the officers of the British Board of Film Classification (BBFC) quizzed parents at the end of a Sunday morning preview. Significantly, she did not ask the children how they perceived it, and only spoke to the adults, but their reaction was sufficient to cause heavy cuts to be made. In the United States the heart-snatch was allowed to remain, but the Motion Picture Association of America (MPAA) introduced a new rating, PG–13, amounting to a strong caution to parents that some material could be disturbing to children younger than thirteen. It was invoked for another Spielberg production, the bizarre comedy *Gremlins*, directed by Joe Dante, in which hundreds of grotesque little creatures of mischievous intent run amok in the usual Spielbergian middle-American community, and are fought by the humans, who wipe them out in kitchen blenders or in the microwave, which lead to cries that such drastic behaviour could become imitative.

Spielberg, after the departure of Amy Irving, had spent time in various short-term relationships, including one with Barbra Streisand which, had it lasted, would have presented a clash of talent on an heroic scale. She was about to direct *Yentl* and listened eagerly to his advice, although later would give short shrift to anyone who suggested that it was not all her unaided work. During *Indiana Jones and the Temple of Doom* Spielberg and Kate Capshaw had become mutually attracted. Born in Forth Worth, Texas, raised in St Louis and educated at the University of Missouri, she was not Jewish, but came from Methodist stock. She had also already been married and had a small daughter. But just as the affair with Spielberg was beginning to look serious Amy Irving returned to his life, and in a touching reunion at an airport, they were together again. She was soon pregnant, and five months after their son Max was born they married, in Santa Fe on 27 November 1985. The dumped Kate Capshaw had, after her rival's reappearance, to continue bravely working on the film, but she had not given up on her chances.

Amblin Entertainment, the production company formed in partnership with his long-term associates Frank Marshall and Kathleen Kennedy, was given impressive new headquarters on the Universal lot, Spielberg having moved away from Warner at Burbank. There had been a suggestion that he should take over the bungalow complex that had been occupied by Alfred Hitchcock, but Spielberg achieved something far better, a New Mexico-style compound with offices for thirty people, with a two-storey pink adobe structure surrounding a garden courtyard fountain, a tranquil oasis in the middle of the functional industrial sheds that comprise a Los Angeles film studio. Amblin had cutting rooms, conference and dining rooms, a chef and a kitchen, a luxurious screening room and Spielberg's sanctum, full of Indian rugs, Norman Rockwell originals and roughly hewn wooden beams that had been artificially distressed. There was not, claimed Spielberg, a true straight line to be found. Along the corridor leading to his office hung famous film posters and framed call-sheets from *Citizen Kane*, and even a Rosebud sled (uncharred) which Spielberg had bought at a Sotheby's sale for $60,500 was on display. From the outside, disregarding the Amblin motif of ET in the basket of Elliott's bicycle, which had been inset in the wall, the impression was of a superior small resort hotel in the desert, but John Milius wickedly described it as 'the biggest Taco Bell in the world'. The cost of the complex, its design heavily influenced by Amy Irving, who had totally succumbed to the charm of Santa Fe, was alleged to be $6 million, but as a proportion of his profitability was a bagatelle.

Indiana Jones and the Temple of Doom, **the follow up to** Raiders of the Lost Ark

12 A Woman's Struggle

The arrival of his son and his marriage altered Spielberg's perspectives. A new home in Pacific Palisades, also decorated in New Mexico style was, under Amy Spielberg's influence, rationed to only two television sets, a deprivation that hitherto he would have found unconscionable. There were still many Norman Rockwell paintings on his walls, however. Rockwell, the foremost American magazine illustrator of the twentieth century, and a chronicler of an idyllic, vanished life, has gained artistic stature in recent years, partly through Spielberg's championing. The fine Norman Rockwell Museum, on a hill outside the old town of Stockbridge in West Massachusetts, in the Berkshires, where the artist spent his later years, was part-funded by Spielberg.

In the new relatively television-free environment Spielberg even began to read, rather than watch, abandoning the habits of a lifetime. He was, it would seem, embarking on a new phase of his career and, as his fortieth birthday approached, anxious to gain credentials as a film-maker who could turn to dramatic subjects with the same skill that he had embraced whimsical fantasy and adolescent adventure.

The book that he turned to was an unlikely one, his first attempt at a woman's story. Alice Walker had won the 1983 Pulitzer prize for *The Color Purple*, a slender but painful and passionate account of the hardships endured by a black woman in the south in the first part of the twentieth century. It was written in epistolary form from a feminist viewpoint, a story of courage and endurance, of strong-willed women victimized by brutal, insensitive men. Quincy Jones, black America's Renaissance man, was all for Spielberg and was happy to write the music. Kathleen Kennedy gave full encouragement to his change of course as a career move. Alice Walker herself had, as it happened, only seen a part of one of Spielberg's movies, but it was the only theatrical one to have an underlying dramatic theme, *The Sugarland Express*. At the first meeting she was impressed by his grasp of what her book was about, and was entirely won over. The fact that he was Jewish even gave him racial empathy, especially when he remembered the occasional anti-Semitism he faced as an adolescent.

The central figure in *The Color Purple*, Celie, gives birth as a young teenager in 1909 to two children, both the progenies of her own father. She is married off to a violent brute she is obliged to call 'Mister' who despises her, and is more interested in her sister Nettie. Her children are taken from her and she faces years of drudgery and despair, while her husband prevents communication between the sisters by suppressing their letters. Years later she discovers that Nettie went to Africa with a missionary group, taking the children with her. Celie then finds happiness with a bisexual lover of her husband, an over-the-hill blues singer called Shug with whom she has a warm lesbian relationship. From it she draws the strength that enables her finally to overcome her husband and claim her life as her own. However harrowing the main story, it ends on an up note of triumph.

The screenplay was written by the Dutch-born Menno Meyjes, his first big feature. He was the third choice after Alice Walker herself had tried but retired after one draft, having become fatigued from the media attention that she had attracted after winning the Pulitzer, and Melissa Matheson had been approached but had not been able to feel compatible with the subject. Even though she was not the screenwriter, Walker exerted a considerable influence on the script.

The casting was crucial and surprising. Two black women from other fields, a stand-up comedian and a local television-show host, were engaged, both to go on to phenomenal success. Whoopi Goldberg, who was signed to play the grown-up Celie (Desreta Jackson plays her as a teenager) was performing her one-woman comedy show in a small San Francisco club, and had never been before a film camera. Walker had seen her and noted the versatility with which she slipped easily into a wide range of characters, and told Spielberg. He invited her to perform the act exclusively for him in the Amblin screening room. It turned out to be full of interested onlookers, including Quincy Jones and Michael Jackson, and she was apprehensive that Spielberg would take offence at one of her pieces which sent up ET as a dope addict. She so impressed him that he urged her to play the leading role. The part of the doughty friend Sofia who is sent to prison for hitting a man, which Goldberg had imagined was the one she was up for, was given to Oprah Winfrey, a former television reporter who had just started to host *AM–Chicago*, a talk show that was attracting attention for its upfront approach to controversial subjects. Her quick-witted intelligence and mettle impressed him.

The pivotal male role of 'Mister' was given to Danny Glover, an experienced actor from a theatrical background who had made his film début six years earlier in *Escape from Alcatraz*. The part of the blues singer, Shug, presented problems. Tina Turner was asked but refused, and Diana Ross was one of those mentioned as a possible. To Alice Walker's relief, having feared that a superstar from the music world would unbalance the film, the part went to Margaret Avery, a reliable character actress whose singing was dubbed.

Goldberg, at sea on a movie set, and initially finding problems working with the others who knew their way around, enjoyed a special rapport with Spielberg, who patiently coached her in the art of playing to the camera. Their mutual understanding was founded to some extent on the fact that she, like him, was a movie buff, and would instantly cotton on when he made reference to past performances that would mean little to those not in the know. Thus he was able to tell her to give him something of the quality of Ingrid Bergman in a particular scene in *Gaslight* or Ray Milland in *The Lost Weekend*, and she would know instantly what he meant. Others in the distinguished black cast included Adolph Caesar, Carl Anderson, Laurence Fishburne and Rae Dawn Chong. Dana Ivey made her début in the white role of the upright employer of the Winfrey character.

Apart from the scenes filmed in Africa, Spielberg, following the precedent of *ET The Extra-Terrestrial*, did not storyboard the action in the interests of performance spontaneity, and there were constant alterations to the script. Spielberg's own expression for the approach he was taking was that he was 'winging it'. What showed on the screen gave no such indication. The cinematography of Allen Daviau was polished and smooth, and he and Spielberg took so much care over the lighting it could have been a William Wyler film. The downside of the perfectionist approach was that it had the effect of sanitizing the squalor of black rural life with a picturesque Hollywood gloss, and much hostile criticism was directed at the prettiness of the North Carolina locations that somehow seemed more appropriate to a heart-warming all-black musical than to a trenchant drama on the human struggle.

It was to prove a bitter lesson for Spielberg, having tried so hard to change the way in which he was perceived, that he should now be attacked for attempting such a serious film. The critics were polarized, some finding the idea that the director of *ET* should attempt a study of a black lesbian as meretricious in itself, as though McDonald's had started to serve lobster thermidor. The lesbian community felt he had soft-pedalled the book's homosexual content, while some black groups, including branches of the National Association for the Advancement of Coloured People (NAACP) found that the depiction of the black male was stereotypical, negative and degrading. It is certainly true that within the two-and-a-half-hour's running time of *The Color Purple* he failed to provide much of the historical background of change, and that in order to secure a PG-13 rating, enabling a larger audience to see it, he downplayed the sexual side of the story. Many of the attacks, however, were directed at him simply for being white and therefore inevitably insensitive to the plight of black Americans.

As usual, in spite of eleven nominations for *The Color Purple*, he was ignored in the Oscar race, and treated with cold suspicion by his fellow directors in the Academy. There was no nomination for best director, although earlier he had received the DGA award, which was usually an automatic indicator that an Oscar would follow. To compound this Academy slighting, on Oscar night, in spite of its eleven nominations, *The Color Purple* did not gain a single statuette. It was as if Spielberg was being punished, first for being too successful, then for his chutzpah in making a film that some saw as a deliberate attempt to solicit the vote. Quite often box-office success is a key requisite for an Academy Award, and many worthy films have been overlooked because they made no impact with the public. But the criterion was met in this instance. Spielberg's film had grossed $90 million in the United States and an impressive $143 million overall, and was among the hits of the year. The continuing rebuffs of the Academy rankled, and many fellow craftsmen felt unease and embarrassment over the attitudes of some of their colleagues, who had ganged up to stop Spielberg, now a considerable force in producing as well as directing.

Some of the films he had originated from Amblin with other directors had been indifferent, including Richard Donner's noisy kid flick *The Goonies*, and Richard Benjamin's homeowners' nightmare, *The Money Pit*. Others had fared better. Robert Zemeckis's effervescent time-warp comedy *Back to the Future* was one of the big hits of 1985 and was to have two sequels. The ingenious adventure yarn *Young Sherlock Holmes*, written by Chris Columbus and directed by Barry Levinson, brought the spirit of *Indiana Jones* and typical Spielberg–Lucas special effects to mid-Victorian London. An animated feature by Don Bluth, *An American Tail*, in which a mouse emigrates to the United States after fleeing from persecution in Tsarist Russia, could have been the story of Spielberg's grandfather, who had reached America following the diaspora. His association with all these films was made clear in the publicity for them, and his name was evoked as a selling tool. Arguably confusion could have resulted, with members of the public, often unaware of the distinction between producing and directing credits, regarding these products as deriving from Spielberg in exactly the same way as *Close Encounters of the Third Kind* and *ET The Extra-Terrestrial*, and in some cases they were profoundly disappointed. A foray into a television series, *Amazing Stories*, a souped-up *Twilight Zone* derivative, was a failure, having promised more than it could deliver, in spite of a formidable roster of starry names and the use of several novices to direct its various segments who later became prominent, and it was attacked for the arrogance and autocratic style which Spielberg had employed to browbeat NBC. The anti-Spielberg faction like to note that his apparent desire to have his name emblazoned all over the place was yet another manifestation of his compulsive megalomania.

The first two segments of *Amazing Stories* Spielberg directed himself, imposing his customary conditions of secrecy to the extent that not only were journalists barred from the set, but he also refused to allow preview tapes to be sent out, fuelling antagonism in the press and the feeling that he would have to deliver something truly exceptional to get away with such an aloof attitude. When the first episode aired on 29 September 1985 expectations were high, but at the same time detractors were waiting to attack. The half-hour story *Ghost Train* starred Roberts Blossom as an old man and Lukas Haas as his young grandson. The old man has been brought back to the country district of his childhood where his son and daughter-in-law have built a new house in the middle of a field. He tells them that the house is fine, but it is in the wrong place. Later he takes his grandson for a walk and they find protruding from the ground a singular American artefact, a railroad spike. The old man tells the boy that seventy-five years ago a railway line ran right across the field, straight through where the house now stands. There was a terrible train wreck after a small boy, waiting for it to come, had put his ear to the track and, because it was a hot day and he was overtired, had fallen into a deep sleep. When some hours later the train eventually came he did not hear the whistle, and the engineer braked so hard to avoid him that it came off the tracks. The boy woke to see a disaster happening fifty feet in front of him. The boy was of course the grandfather, and he announces confidently that the train is going to come again that night, and this time he will board it. The boy believes him, but his parents think the old man has become senile and have him sedated. Then, during the night, the whistle is heard, and the bright headlight is seen in the distance, increasing in intensity as the house begins to shake. The parents rush downstairs to find that an enormous steam locomotive, its bell clanging, is pulling into their living room, demolishing everything in its path. Inside the first coach are people in old-fashioned clothes, and the conductor tells the old man it is time, at long last, for him to board. It steams away with him never to return, leaving the bemused houseowners wondering how they are going to explain the large hole through their brand-new home to the insurance company.

A whimsical tale, it bore plenty of Spielbergian characteristics: the small boy who has more understanding than the adults, the bright lights in the night and the shaking house to portend an abnormal visitation, and the regard for the old man who could have been Spielberg's own grandfather Fievel. As photographed by Allen Daviau, it had far more visual polish than was normal in most hastily assembled segments for television series. The spectacular eruption of the locomotive into the house was diminished on television, but signified that a huge sum, of $1 million, had been expended on a mere half-hour of programming. It went largely unsung by the reviewers, some of whom claimed that Spielberg was diluting his talent. 'What was so amazing about that?' was the question asked by the *Washington Post* television critic.

The second of the *Amazing Stories* series, again directed by Spielberg himself, compounded the lukewarm reaction. A wartime aviation story about a B–17 crew stationed in England, it was called *The Mission*. The seasoned captain, played by Kevin Costner, has a special regard for the midships belly gunner (Casey Siemaszko), who amuses the entire crew by drawing cartoons, and has an ambition to take his pregnant wife to California where he can work for Walt Disney. Their bombing raid on Germany is fraught, and they are engaged by several Me109s. The tail gunner shoots one of them down, but a section of the exploding fighter hits the Flying Fortress, embedding itself over the hatch covering the lower gun turret, which is a Perspex bubble protruding from the aircraft's underside. The gunner crammed within it cannot get out and is obliged to wait until they make their return to base when the oxyacetylene cutters can be deployed. Slowly it dawns on him and the crew that the undercarriage has been shot away, and that the only way the captain can bring the plane in is by a wheels-up crash-landing. The gunner is doomed, and the flight home is a journey to his inevitable death, greatly affecting his crew colleagues and his wretched captain. Then as the airfield is in sight and the padre is saying prayers over the control tower intercom a miracle occurs. The gunner draws a cartoon of the stricken plane and adds a pair of prominent wheels, and entreats the captain to try to lower the landing gear one more time. From each nacelle a bright yellow cartoon wheel on a candy-striped stalk plops into place, enabling the aircraft to make a safe landing and the gunner, who is in an ecstatic trance, to be cut free. With everyone at a safe distance, Costner wakes him up. The cartoon wheels melt away, and the B–17 sinks on to the tarmac in a clattering heap.

Such a stupid story, even from Spielberg's fevered imagination, was insulting to the intelligence. Yet it was invested with massive production values, a star-laden cast, stylish photography and lavish special effects more normally associated with feature films. It was also expanded from the usual half-hour slot to fill an hour of television time, and was released outside the United States as part of a triple bill of segments, the others respectively directed by Robert Zemeckis and William Dear, under the title *Amazing Stories: the Movie*. Although the television series limped on, it never ignited viewer enthusiasm, and quietly died after twenty-six films had been made. On the positive side, and to its credit it introduced the directing talents of Joe Dante, Phil Joanou and Kevin Reynolds as well as big names such as Eastwood and Scorsese and was a forcing house for new talent, and many of those involved in the programmes went on to impressive careers.

13 'The Cadillac of the Skies'

After *The Color Purple* Spielberg's appraisal of strands of contemporary literature continued. The next book that Spielberg wanted to direct was J. G. Ballard's autobiographical novel *Empire of the Sun*, which describes the experiences of a British teenage boy who, having lived a privileged existence in Shanghai, is separated from his parents by the Japanese and held in various camps until the liberation. Something similar had happened to Ballard himself, although he had not been separated from his parents, a central theme of the book. Originally it had been a production project that Spielberg had hoped that David Lean, who had made a return to the screen after a long absence with *A Passage to India*, would direct. Lean's gestation period for films was legendarily lengthy, and after a year of failing to see a way to do it he passed up the project in order to start thinking about Joseph Conrad's *Nostromo* instead, which again Spielberg was to produce, although at a later stage a falling-out and a parting occurred. Lean continued elsewhere to prepare *Nostromo* until his death in 1991.

Among Spielberg's early film memories was *The Bridge on the River Kwai*, Lean's massive 1957 epic in which the cultures clash between the Japanese imperial invader and the British defenders of empire is symbolized by the uneasy interaction of a prison-camp commandant and the senior officer among the captors. Lean's film was a significant influence on Spielberg's desire to take on the direction of *Empire of the Sun* himself. In Ballard's book the boy, a brat at the beginning, learns to survive the camps on his wits, and emerges as clever and self-sufficient to a fine degree. Spielberg immediately spotted an *Oliver Twist* connection, and one of the strong characters in the film is the American merchant seaman Basie, played by John Malkovich, who as a surrogate parent teaches him life's basic principle, which is to do everything possible to avoid getting caught.

It was to be an epic production, lit by Allen Daviau, and filmed at Elstree and on location, including three weeks of shooting in Shanghai itself, where the Bund, the pre-war waterfront financial enclave where

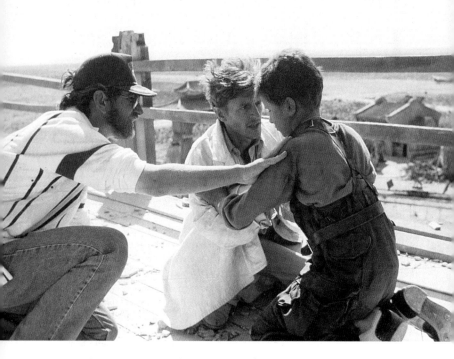

Empire of the Sun: **Christian Bale (right, with Spielberg)**
was chosen from more than 4,000 young actors for the lead.
His electrifying performance was said to surpass even that
of Jean-Pierre Léaud in Truffaut's Les Quatre Cent Coups.

western banking architecture flourished, had altered little in the intervening years. Permission was granted for three weeks of filming there, the
first time that a Hollywood film company had been allowed in since the
Maoist revolution. The luxurious international settlement mansions had,
under communism, been converted into multiple apartments and were less
suitable for filming, but Spielberg noted their similarity to the large 1930s
houses that could be found south-west of London in salubrious areas such
as Virginia Water, St George's Hill and Sunningdale. The Japanese prison-
camp scenes were shot near Jerez in southern Spain, where an airstrip for
various vintage aircraft formed part of the huge outdoor set.

The planes were an important element. The boy, Jim Graham, is
obsessed by them. His pre-war bedroom is crammed with models
suspended from the ceiling, and in an interlude during a fancy-dress
party he wanders off in an Ali Baba costume and comes across a crashed
Japanese fighter in a field. Climbing into the cockpit, he imagines himself
as an ace. When he is in the camp, he dreams incessantly of the freedom
of flight and endlessly exchanges aircraft facts with Basie. Towards the
end of the war he witnesses the ritual ceremonials undergone by kamikaze
pilots as they prepare for their suicide missions, and salutes these
absurdly courageous young men, even though they are Japanese and
therefore the enemy. Then, shortly before the Americans finally liberate
the camp, a squadron of P–51 Mustangs streams in and strafes the adjacent airfield, and in the midst of the terror as bullets fly, in a beautiful, if
impossible moment, the pilot of one of the gleaming aircraft slowly waves
at the boy, who shouts, delirious with glee, 'P–51, Cadillac of the skies'.

Casting was difficult. Jim had to age convincingly from eleven to fifteen
and to undergo changes in personality that were not all to do with the
onset of adolescence. A thirteen-year-old was picked after an extensive
search through 4,000 possible choices over a period of nine months.
Christian Bale had actually acted with Amy Irving in a television production, *Anastasia: the Mystery of Anna*, in which he had played Alexis, the
Tsar's haemophiliac son. He proved to be a brilliant choice, and when
the film was released Andrew Sarris in the *Village Voice* claimed that his
electrifying performance even surpassed that of Jean-Pierre Léaud in
Truffaut's *Les Quatre Cents Coups*.

The screenplay by Tom Stoppard was unusually devoid of sentimentality for a Spielberg work, and remained in tune with Ballard's original
account, although much of the imagery connected with aircraft was
injected by the director. The danger skirted by Spielberg throughout is
connected with the ambiguity of the leading character, who is hardly off
the screen. His initial behaviour is scarcely endearing. He is a pampered
child of wealthy parents, his father a businessman who has made a
good living from Asia. His son is used to getting his own way, and is

hermetically sealed off from the outside world. His appreciation of the political implications of the impending disaster is, even in a schoolboy, near zero. He is far more interested in the details of respective performances of aircraft. Spielberg brilliantly conveys the chaos of war, the panic evacuations, the streets crammed with thousands and, above all, the pain of separation in a hopelessly unyielding crowd, an emotion to which he was able to give full strength. Jim is parted from his parents because he drops his model plane, and in retrieving it lets go of his mother's hand. In a trice she has been swallowed up by the multitude.

The learning process that he has to face is painful. The house has been taken over by the Japanese, and he finds the previously docile servants looting it. Later, after having been a prisoner of the Japanese, Jim has grown older and infinitely wiser, and has survived to exercise an unhealthy degree of power, having become as calculating and manipulative as his Faginesque mentor Basie who eventually overreaches himself and is destroyed. Towards the end there is an apocalyptic flash in the sky. It is the atomic bomb that fell on Nagasaki, effectively the termination of the war, the symbol of a drastic victory. At the reunion with his mother in a collective group of adults and children it takes time for them to recognize each other.

In some respects the bleakness of *Empire of the Sun* seems to suggest a dry run for *Schindler's List*, which was to be a superior work dramatically. Both Jim Graham and Oskar Schindler learn how to exploit the enemy and turn it into the means of staying alive. But *Empire of the Sun*, for all its epic grandeur and visual magnificence, its controlled performances and fine soundtrack, especially the haunting hymn 'Suo Gan', sung by the Ambrosian Singers, is less clear in its intention than *Schindler's List*, even ending on an empty note, as though the experience of war is all about survival in extreme and testing conditions, and after that peace can only be an anticlimax.

The film was received lukewarmly by the public, and it grossed only $67 million worldwide, which by Spielberg standards can be deemed a failure, with even *1941* achieving considerably better results. He had taken care to avoid the usual accusation that he was sentimentally exploiting the essence of childhood by making Jim a rounded, flawed character, but now he was castigated for plunging a young hero into a realistic milieu of viciousness and sadism. Conversely, some reviewers thought that, as in *The Color Purple*, he had sanitized reality, reduced the extent of the privations, and even made some aspects of camp life enjoyable. Ballard, however, who had lived through similar experiences, was well satisfied. The story was told from Jim's perspective, and he knew that children had a resilience and ability to endure that was lost by adults. How else would Victorians who went on to rule the world have stood up as children to the Spartan conditions in nineteenth-century public schools?

14 Chipping Off the Old Block

Although the Academy gave Spielberg the Irving G. Thalberg Memorial Award, an honorary prize often bestowed on eminences such as Alfred Hitchcock and Cary Grant who never managed the Oscar proper, it was with the now predictable inevitability of a foregone conclusion that *Empire of the Sun*, having received six nominations (none for best director or best picture) did not pick up a single award on the night. That its box-office performance had been somewhat indifferent would certainly not have helped its chances. The two serious pictures he had made in a row had weakened his grip on popular taste, but another *Indiana Jones* instalment could regain it. To do so meant yielding *Rain Man*, a project on which he had been working with Dustin Hoffman, in which the actor was to play an autistic patient who is a remarkable idiot savant. Barry Levinson inherited it and the finished film went on to win Oscars for Hoffman and Levinson, for its screenplay and as best picture.

The Nazis were back for *Indiana Jones and the Last Crusade*, for which the screenplay was written by Jeffrey Boam. It also introduced the hero's father in a leading role. Harrison Ford was to find himself acting alongside Sean Connery, playing another archaeologist who, as an obsessive scholar, is even more resolute and daring than his offspring. The quest was to be for the most famous missing artefact in legend, literature and Christendom. At the suggestion of George Lucas, it was nothing less than the Holy Grail, the cup used at the Last Supper and later to collect the blood of Jesus, which was supposed to have been spirited away by Joseph of Arimathea. Had it not been for the Monty Python team, who had usurped it for their 1975 film, the Holy Grail would have been part of the title. The Grail allegedly has the power of eternal life, and, when it is finally located, it turns out to be guarded by a formidable but centuries-old crusader. It is naturally sought by the Nazis, intent on ensuring that the 'thousand-year Reich' will have an immortal Führer leading it. The female lead is weak in comparison with Karen Allen and Kate Capshaw in the earlier films, another blonde, played by Alison Doody, who turns out to be a German spy, and also to have had a fling with both father and son. The racist implications of the first two films are missing, replaced by the intrusion of unwholesome aspects of Nazism including a book-burning sequence. Hitler himself even has a walk-on appearance, and gives Jones Senior his autograph. The set-piece action sequences are as effective and thrilling as any that have gone before, and include a Zeppelin scene and a desert chase with a huge Panzer tank.

The film starts in 1912, with River Phoenix playing the young Indy on an expedition in Utah, an enjoyably silly adventure that leads to his acquisition of his trademarks, the bullwhip and the fedora hat. So successful was the idea that it led to a popular Amblin television series, *Young Indiana Jones*.

As with the two preceding films the home base was Elstree Studios, which had undergone difficulties since the *Temple of Doom*. Then the studios had been owned by EMI, but subsequently they had been sold on to Cannon who, after financial difficulties, offloaded them again to a London financial consortium. The new owners' intention was to level the site for homes and shopping. Spielberg for a while considered buying them himself, but after joining in a campaign that included lobbying the House of Commons he was delighted that a preservation order was served. Eventually half the site became a Tesco superstore, and the rest was acquired by the local authority, Hertsmere, to be retained for film-making.

The overseas locations were in Italy and Petra, Jordan, as well as Almeria, Spain, which represented the Jordanian desert. Somewhat surprisingly there was a lengthy sequence in the catacombs of Venice, which of course have yet to be discovered, and would probably be extremely waterlogged.

The last *Indiana Jones* film to date holds up against its predecessors on account of the interplay between Connery and Ford. The latter, grace-fully sliding into middle age, hardly merited the patronizing use of the term 'junior', and some of the bantering dialogue was ad-libbed by the actors who worked well together. Connery came across as though he had not enjoyed himself so much since the days when he defined James Bond for the screen. Spielberg was able to reflect that the film was a satisfying money-spinner, with a worldwide gross of $495 million.

15 Can Heaven Wait?

In spite of denials, Spielberg's marriage to Amy Irving was foundering. Monumental wealth, and with it several palatially luxurious homes, including a penthouse in the Trump Tower in New York that was even loftier than that of Andrew Lloyd Webber, were not enough to compensate for inordinately long separations when Spielberg was filming. She had involuntarily passed up on her acting career to be a wife and mother. Not only had she not appeared in any of his films, apart from a minor role in the first of the television *Amazing Stories* segments that he had directed himself, and as the singing voice of the cartoon character Jessica Rabbit in the ingenious live-action and animation combination directed by Robert Zemeckis, *Who Framed Roger Rabbit*, she found that her position as his wife was actually a disincentive to other directors. They were uneasy in allowing someone so close to him on their productions. The only notable film she made during her time as his wife was *Crossing Delancey*, directed by Joan Micklin Silver, in which she played an unmarried thirtyish Jewish woman in New York whose mother has engaged a matchmaker to find a husband.

The divorce was announced in April 1989, with custody of Max to be shared. The settlement under Californian law would have been enormous, equivalent to half of Spielberg's wealth which would have been above $200 million. Meanwhile Kate Capshaw had returned to his side and was his partner for the London première of *Indiana Jones and the Last Crusade* in June of that year. In 1990 she gave birth to his child, a daughter, Sasha, and after converting to the Jewish faith she married him on his Long Island estate on 12 October 1991.

One of the films of the 1940s that had attracted Spielberg from a young age, having seen it on late-night television, was a wartime romantic fantasy directed by Victor Fleming. In *A Guy Named Joe* Spencer Tracy plays a bomber pilot who is killed in action, leaving his girl (Irene Dunne), who also flies, heartbroken. In heaven he is assigned to be the guardian angel of a young pilot (Van Johnson) whom he then invisibly guides through flying school and into combat. His newly acquired angelic disposition is severely rattled when Johnson and Dunne fall for each other, and he has to learn that the supreme test of love is knowing when to let go. A sentimental hit, in spite of the absurd storyline and its representation of heaven as a place where people wade around with clouds of dry ice covering their ankles, it had resonances for all those who were involved in the experience of wartime, with its dislocations and the possibility of sudden death and bereavement. As far as Spielberg was concerned there was a point of identity in the strain of the relationship of his own parents, and his inability, like the Spencer Tracy character, to do anything about it.

He decided to embark on a remake. The screenplay of *A Guy Named Joe* had been written by Dalton Trumbo, an accomplished hand who shortly after the war suffered imprisonment and blacklisting for refusing to tell the notorious House Un-American Activities Committee whether or not he had been a Communist. This film and several others that he had written during the war were carefully scrutinized for subversive themes. The screenwriter for the Spielberg film, to be called *Always*, was Jerry Belson, but Trumbo, who died in 1976, was to be given a generous screen credit. Richard Dreyfuss, like Spielberg, regarded *A Guy Named Joe* as one of his favourite films, and claimed to have seen it thirty-five times. When they were making *Jaws* he and Spielberg would enliven periods of boredom by quoting dialogue from it line by line. The project simmered on the back burner for a number of years, going through several draft screenplays, until at last it came to the fore. Dreyfuss had desperately wanted to play the Tracy role, although Spielberg had been thinking in terms of a more conventional male lead such as Paul Newman or Robert Redford, who were both interested. Eventually he caved in to Dreyfuss's entreaties. For the Irene Dunne role he cast Holly Hunter, attracted by her feisty qualities, and as the young pilot a newcomer, Brad Johnson. The large and likable John Goodman was to be the best friend, and the role of the angel who invests Dreyfuss in his task, after Sean Connery had proved unavailable, he gave to Audrey Hepburn, who appeared clad entirely in white, and sadly making her last screen appearance.

The film is miscalculated on more than one front. It seems a serious error to have discarded the World War Two background and updated it so that the fliers are the hard-bitten professional pilots who make a living dowsing forest fires in mountain states such as Montana, where it was shot. They may well be a rugged breed, but it is hard to feel an emotional involvement with them, since their calling, unlike that of wartime servicemen, is entirely of their own choosing. Nevertheless, in spite of the modern setting, they fly slow, ancient, piston-engined crates of 1940s vintage, listen to old sentimental songs as they drink their beer and clown around in the bar, and talk to each other in dated slang. Holly

Hunter is a tomboy type, who can sink her liquor with the best of them, and when she has a row with Dreyfuss she cools off by climbing into a cockpit and zooming into the air to engage in a few hairy passes over the field until she has simmered down. When she exchanges her ratty flying gear for what she calls 'girl clothes' the entire assembly of tough airmen and mechanics falls apart in stupefied amazement.

The second miscalculation is the casting. Spencer Tracy was popular because he could be relied on to deliver solid 'honest Joe' performances. Significantly his character in *A Guy Named Joe* is actually called Pete. The name Joe was colloquially used in the USAAF to indicate a regular guy. Dreyfuss, a much more complex actor than Tracy, conveys too many layers to his performance, as well as a cynicism that was not present in the original. Similarly, Holly Hunter lacks the cool presence of Irene Dunne, but brought with her a bagful of neurotic hangups that make her character harder to fathom, and often seems to border on the hysterical. Brad Johnson is weak and insipid as the young pilot, too inexperienced to be much more than a conventionally handsome comic-book idea of how a young pilot should look, and one of the screenplay's serious embarrassments is to make him at one point attempt to imitate John Wayne, so grotesquely that even Holly Hunter could have made a better job of it. Of the main characters only John Goodman is entirely satisfactory, and brings sympathy to his best-pal role, the unwitting cause of Pete's death. He flies too close to the flames and his aircraft catches fire. Pete zooms after him in his plane, dowses the flames but crashes, and finds himself in a paradisiacal forest glade with Audrey Hepburn, his personal angel, one of the improvements on the old film where heaven was aswirl with its dry ice, and such matters as admission procedure were conducted with military decorum.

Dreyfuss has died without declaring his love, or if he did, the noise of his engines drowned out his words. Consequently there are two reasons why he must relinquish Dorinda, the Hunter character. In the first place he has failed to let her know what she has wanted to hear, and in the second he is now somewhat inconveniently dead. Yet he cannot quit, and he hovers around invisibly agonizing while the Brad Johnson character makes his pitch for her and she seems to respond. Only when the running time has begun to mount ominously does he reach the conclusion that the audience would have expected from the moment his plane is destroyed and he loses his life. He realizes at long last that he must surrender her to the living, but not until he has first been responsible for saving her from death, by instilling in her the will to survive after she has crashed on a firefighting mission and is drowning in a lake.

Spielberg's film is unabashed schlock, albeit mounted superbly. Yet the flying sequences are vivid and realistic, with footage of real forest fires integrated cleverly and seamlessly. As a love story it is hopelessly unsatisfying by modern standards. There was a vogue in the 1940s for films of this kind, where the dead and the living faced up to each other as fate intervened. The best of them, and having the most influence on the directors of Spielberg's generation, was Michael Powell and Emeric Pressburger's *A Matter of Life and Death*, or as it was called in the version that he knew in America, *Stairway to Heaven*, in which an American girl radio operator makes a plea before a celestial court for the life of an RAF bomber pilot with whom she fell in love during his last minutes on his doomed aircraft. In wartime the experience of grief was an ever-present possibility for all those whose loved ones were on active service in combat areas. A belief in the hereafter, and that the dead could watch over the living, was a source of comfort for many thousands of people. Hence the popularity of such ideas on the screen. It soon passed, and by the late 1980s the notion looked ludicrous. Not surprisingly, Spielberg's film was unsuccessful, grossing a mere $77 million world-wide, which for Spielberg was plainly a flop. Curiously, following *Always* other film-makers took up the idea, and used it as a basis for comedy, most successfully in the case of Jerry Zucker and *Ghost*, and Robert Zemeckis for *Death Becomes Her*.

Why did Spielberg call his film *Always*? Pete and Dorinda, in the best lovers' tradition, had their tune which they constantly dance to or hum. In the first film it was the poignant ballad 'I'll Get By (As Long as I Have You)'. Spielberg preferred to use the classic Irving Berlin song 'Always'. Unfortunately the prickly little composer, by then in his mid-nineties, refused to allow it to be used and was so rich that money made no difference, and that was that. So Spielberg gave up, and instead substituted the haunting melody 'Smoke Gets in Your Eyes' by Jerome Kern (deceased in 1946), which is repetitively, if not incessantly, sung on the soundtrack by The Platters. He could hardly use the title *Smoke Gets in Your Eyes* for a film in which courageous forest firefighters get killed. So it was to remain *Always*, even though there was another film doing the rounds just before it which had the same title. The earlier work was written, produced and directed by Henry Jaglom, an independent film-maker who had a few years before he castigated Spielberg within the Directors' Guild for making *The Color Purple*, declaring that the result was as if Disney had decided to direct *The Grapes of Wrath*. Perhaps Spielberg was now quietly exacting a minor revenge.

16 Straight On to Morning

The adolescent naivety of *Always* indicated Spielberg's unease with grown-up romance. Pursuing the logic of the recurring criticism that he had somehow resisted full adulthood and that most of his films were viewed through the eyes of the young, he further fulfilled it by turning for his next subject to Peter Pan, the boy who was incapable of growing up. The twist he came up with was to visualize what Peter would have been like if that prohibition had no longer prevailed, and he had managed to achieve full adult life. J. M. Barrie's magnificent work had always been at the forefront of his imagination, and it is perhaps a pity that earlier in his career he had never attempted a more straightforward film version. By the time that *Hook* was made Spielberg had become stung by criticism and jaded with success, and could no longer look at *Peter Pan* with the freshness of vision that he had brought to his early career.

There had been a concrete proposal a decade earlier to make *Peter Pan* for Disney, as a live-action counterpart to their cartoon of 1953. I remember raising it with him shortly after he had made *The Color Purple*. He told me that he had now abandoned the idea, and that the reason was the birth of his son Max. 'I now have my Peter Pan,' he said.

Separately, the idea for *Hook* came about through the screenwriter Jim V. Hart and the director Nick Castle, and was under development at TriStar. After Sony bought the company Mike Medavoy, who had been Spielberg's first agent, was installed to run the company, and on finding the screenplay, sent it to him. The studio desperately needed a hit movie, after a succession of costly flops, such as *Hudson Hawk*. Spielberg was immediately interested, which meant that Castle was handsomely paid off and given a story credit, and Hart was named as screenwriter, although other writers were called in to inject more colour, including Malia Scotch Marmo, who received a credit, and Carrie Fisher, who did not. In some quarters it was seen as another instance of Spielberg's arrogance, although Medavoy shouldered the blame himself. The stars were to be Robin Williams as Peter and Dustin Hoffman as his old adversary Captain Hook, who has somehow escaped from the crocodile that was supposed to have terminated him at the end of Barrie's play.

The premise of *Hook* is that Peter Pan had been transformed into Peter Banning, a quintessential figure of the modern age, an American businessman, a corporate merger fixer, perhaps not all that far removed from the character that Michael Douglas plays in Oliver Stone's *Wall Street*, the sort of person who has a mobile phone almost as a permanent extension to his right hand. He is also a father too enveloped in his business deals to turn up in time for his son's little-league baseball game and who misses his daughter's appearance in a school play, a husband too preoccupied to notice his wife's discontent, a workaholic who has relegated his family to the background as an accoutrement of his designer lifestyle. Then he takes them on a trip to London to see the now aged Wendy (Maggie Smith, under half a ton of prosthetics to make her look extraordinarily old), who is being honoured by the Great Ormond Street Children's Hospital. Barrie left the rights to *Peter Pan* to the hospital, and hundreds of thousands of children since, my own son included, have benefited from the wonderful legacy. Wendy, it seems, adopted Peter many years ago and raised him (just how many years ago is not mentioned – Barrie wrote the original play in 1904, and turned it into a novel in 1911, and it has always seemed to belong firmly to the Edwardian era, but by 1991, the year in which the film is set, Wendy would have almost been a centenarian, and the assumption must be that Peter did not start his 'growing up' until the 1950s at the earliest).

In London something strange, but very reminiscent of the old Spielberg, occurs: a mysterious light behind the window, and the children missing the next day as though they could have been abducted by aliens, except that a parchment note reveals that it is the work of Captain Hook. Forgotten memories surface, assisted by Wendy, but more importantly there is a visit from Tinkerbell, played by a seven-inch tall Julia Roberts, who convinces Peter to return with her to Neverland and find the children.

Alas, just as the magic has surfaced so it sinks again. Neverland has the fatigued look of a theme-park attraction nearing the end of its life, and it was rumoured that the sets had been designed with that dual purpose in mind, and could one day be re-erected to make a special *Hook* ride. The Lost Boys have been carefully sifted to ensure, in the interests of political correctness, a balanced ethnicity. Dustin Hoffman's Captain Hook is a moustachioed, gap-toothed buffoon who speaks with a sort of Terry-Thomas plummy accent, while his sidekick Smee (Bob Hoskins) delivers a hammily comic performance rather more suited to a television sitcom.

So many things are wrong with *Hook* that it represents a classic instance of Hollywood hubris. To begin with, the stars, Hoffman and Williams, and the director worked out a deal, brokered by Mike Ovitz's Creative Artists Agency (CAA), to divide up 40 per cent of the gross from all markets, an unprecedented levy on a film's revenue. Julia Roberts received $2.5 million for her small part. The budget escalated from $48 million to $60 million and way beyond. The sets, in spite of their unremarkable look, ate up millions and filled nine sound stages at Sony's Culver City studios, the complex that in the heyday of MGM had accommodated such productions as *Mutiny on the Bounty*, *The Wizard of Oz* and *Singin' in the Rain*. Hook's pirate ship was so big that it could be framed in its entirety only if the camera moved outside, and shot through the stage's open doors. Some of the stars who dropped by to see what was going on were roped in to play cameos. Glenn Close, for instance, was given a beard and plays a pirate, while Phil Collins puts in an appearance as a plain-clothes London inspector, improbably wearing an American-style police badge on his suit.

The usual Spielberg polish is often lacking. The choreography of the sword fights is particularly disappointing, inelegant and unconvincing, while the massed battles of Lost Boys and pirates are confused and messy. At one point such is the carelessness of attention to detail that the camera loses the perspective on the sea horizon on a painted diorama behind the ship so that it appears to tilt almost ninety degrees, although this lapse does not show up on television transmissions. Robin Williams gives a muted, uneasy performance, and his comic persona is kept on a very firm leash, lessening his appeal. Julia Roberts also looks out of place. In one ill-judged moment she confronts Williams as a full-size person rather than miniature sprite, wearing a somewhat flamboyant ball dress. It is almost as if the actress had demanded at least one scene where she could flaunt her glamorous side, having for the rest of her role been confined to an asexual outfit which in any case was hard to appreciate, given her lilliputian condition. Peter's stunned response to her suddenly startling manifestation is to say 'Tinkerbell, you're humongous!'

At the end Peter returns to the real world, having regained his children and bestowed the leadership of the Lost Boys on the pudgiest one in another gesture of political correctness. Far from finding himself, he has exorcized all the old ghosts, and perhaps become a better father.

The overrun on the shooting schedule was forty days, further cause for media speculation that the film was going to be an overblown failure. The press delights in stories of insane extravagance in the film world, and *Hook*, like *Titanic* in 1996 and much of 1997, was viewed as large-scale profligacy, with greed overcoming common sense. There were anxieties before the opening, which turned to horror when some of the reviews were negative. The real test was with the public. Even though it was often reported to be a flop it was not. A truer assessment would have been that it was not an overwhelming success. In the domestic arena it grossed a little over $100 million, but worldwide it attracted some $288 million. On top of that were the sales of videos and other spin-offs. The costly production more than covered itself, which meant that the principals on their 40 per cent deal became very much richer.

Robin Williams gave a muted, uneasy performance in Hook.
**So many things were wrong with the film that it was perceived
as a critical and box-office disaster.**

17 Entry of the Dinosaurs

Spielberg was next to work on two films almost simultaneously. Each, although in different genres, would add to his stature, pushing asunder the negativity that had been associated with the reaction to *Hook*. The first was *Jurassic Park*, the other *Schindler's List*. The latter would be filmed immediately after his version of Michael Crichton's fantasy novel based on the premise that DNA found in an insect embedded in amber could enable the cloning of prehistoric creatures. There was a reason. Steve Ross, the chief executive of Warner and after 1989 the co-chairman of Time–Warner, had been a persuasive friend and staunch patron of Spielberg, and in many respects the most important influence on his career. In 1992 he was dying of cancer, and for that reason Spielberg resolved to make *Jurassic Park* ahead of *Schindler's List*, which would be the most sombre film he had ever made.

Crichton, the author of *Jurassic Park*, armed with a formidable Harvard education in medicine, had become a best-selling novelist by using his scientific knowledge to push credibility one stage further, and had become something of a master of the 'what if?' type of thriller, having made his name with *The Andromeda Strain*. He had also directed a number of imaginative films from his own material himself, including *Westworld* and *The First Great Train Robbery*. Spielberg had already optioned a Crichton screenplay based on his experiences as a medical school intern, which would eventually form the basis for the highly successful TV series, *ER*. He had also read *Jurassic Park* in proof form before it had been published, and the film possibilities had immediately intrigued him. A complication was that both men were represented by CAA who had no qualms about setting a high price, and eventually the film rights were sold for $1.5 million plus a percentage of the gross. Crichton favoured Spielberg over other contenders, and was delighted to be given the opportunity to write his own screenplay, although as was his custom, Spielberg later brought in other writers. For Spielberg it was back to the storyboard as he blocked out the filming of some of the most spectacular sequences. The new film was to make extensive use of computer-generated imagery (CGI), which had moved on a long way from his first experiences with it in *Close Encounters of the Third Kind*, and the new film was destined to set fresh benchmarks in special effects. The decision to move into CGI in order to create realistic prehistoric creatures was taken after Spielberg had been shown by Dennis Murren of Industrial Light & Magic how well the system compared with the cumbersome and more conventional method of using stop-motion models, some of them on a full-size scale. Before *Jurassic Park* James Cameron's *Terminator 2: Judgment Day* had used CGI to create a cyborg made from liquid metal, with the capability of changing shape at will. An even earlier pioneer of the technique was *The Abyss*, another Cameron film released in 1989. After his scrutiny Spielberg needed little convincing that CGI was the way forward. Computers were able not only to recreate the three-dimensional shape of prehistoric creatures but to work out their muscle structure and how they would have moved. Although the accuracy of their conjecture would be difficult to test, even the most sceptical experts were satisfied with the results.

A central character in *Jurassic Park* is a billionaire of a scientific bent who, having discovered the way to clone creatures from prehistory, establishes in secret a theme park, stocked with various kinds of dinosaurs, on a remote Pacific island. The action of the film takes place during a junket-tour in advance of the public, with interested scientists and others flying in to see marvels that mankind has never beheld before, living dinosaurs. Initially it is like a modern variation on the theme of *The Lost World*, an old Conan Doyle yarn, and *King Kong*, a classic film in Spielberg's repertoire of favourites. As in these notable predecessors, man learns a bitter lesson from his interference with nature. The monsters are too strong and indeed too intelligent to be restrained by mere 10,000-volt fences, and after the security systems have been closed down by an employee who is trying to steal valuable embryos, they break loose and begin an orgy of terror and destruction.

The part of John Hammond, the eager billionaire, went to Richard Attenborough, possibly as a grateful gesture for his support on the night that *ET* failed to win an Oscar. After a long and distinguished acting career Attenborough had turned to directing, and with films of an epic sweep such as *A Bridge Too Far*, *Young Winston*, *Gandhi* and *Cry Freedom* had shown a comparable mastery of distended cinematic logistics as possessed by Spielberg. For *Jurassic Park* he returned to screen acting after a fifteen-year hiatus. The character he played was modified from the avaricious megalomaniac in the book to that of a wild-eyed enthusiast, agog with the idea of playing with creation itself, and Attenborough grafted on an Edinburgh accent which had the effect of seeming to enhance his scientific credentials. Other casting included Sam Neill as a brilliant paleontologist, Laura Dern, the botanist in the party who is there to fulfil the female-in-peril role, and Jeff Goldblum, another scientist, and the cynic in the group with a ready wisecrack for every situation, however extraordinary. Neill is not particularly enamoured of the young and is distinctly unhappy that there are two (Joseph Mazzello and Ariana Richards) who as Attenborough's grandchildren are juvenile members of the privileged preview group.

In a sense the human actors found themselves at a disadvantage, outclassed and rendered into pygmies by the simulated prehistoric creatures, which at first glance looked entirely real. The moment in the film when the visitors and the audience first come across a small group of dinosaurs quietly grazing is as wondrous as anything in all of Spielberg's films. Later a leaping herd of deer-like gallimuses stampedes towards the actors in an astonishing CGI sequence that looks totally credible. In some respects the early sequences are more impressive than the later scary ones, when the velociraptors and tyrannosaurs put on a *Godzilla* act and terrorize all the human beings on the island. The last section of the film is entirely destructive, with the administration buildings besieged and laid waste. Spielberg stages a particularly effective cat-and-mouse ritual in a huge kitchen, and with an abrupt edit inflicts a sudden shock on the audience as terrifying as the appearance of the escaped convict Magwitch in Lean's *Great Expectations*, or the knife-slaying of the detective on the staircase in Hitchcock's *Psycho*.

The dinosaurs were not all computer-generated. Some were animatronic miniatures that were sometimes used in conjunction with CGI. The most impressive tyrannosaur model was eighteen feet tall and another massive creation was the sick triceratops that has become ill from eating inappropriate food. By far the most terrifying creatures were the velociraptors which can move at lightning speed and strike with concentrated ferocity. Although the paleontological research was conducted with the thoroughness that only ample funding could support, the scientific establishment later poured scorn on the premise that cloning from a DNA sample millions of years old was remotely possible, and pointed out that the dinosaur specimens in the film ranged from cretaceous to Triassic periods and were therefore non-contemporary with each other by considerable margins. The Jurassic era, like the Triassic, lasted for forty-five million years, but the natural tendency when dinosaurs are discussed is to presume that it all happened at more or less the same time. Hollywood in such absurdities as *One Million BC* even had prehistoric man seen to be living at that same time that the great beasts walked the Earth. It is a typical example of the power of cinema to create myths. In the case of *Jurassic Park* so much worldwide interest in dinosaurs was aroused that museums of prehistory suddenly found a manifold and perplexing increase in popularity.

As if to anticipate the spin-off potential of the film its logos and promotional image were already in place before filming began and are actually an element within it, with a glimpse of all the merchandising awaiting sale to those who have made the journey to Jurassic Park. The tour is meant to be taken in a range of specially adapted Ford cars, and the exhortation to stay inside at all times is constantly iterated, an instruction that is naturally ignored. In any case, when the creatures turn nasty the small vehicles are found to be dangerously vulnerable, and are destroyed as easily as a schoolboy tramples flat an old tin can.

The location shooting took place on the Hawaiian island of Kauai, and even though towards the end of the time a fierce hurricane struck and 130-miles-per-hour winds caused severe damage to the hotel in which most of the cast and crew were staying, Spielberg was able to adhere to the schedule, and even complete ahead of time.

The film opened as the summer blockbuster of 1993. The consensual view of the critics was that the breathtaking effects, particularly the use of CGI, far outweighed the deficiencies of a very basic storyline and the two-dimensional characterization. The use of children as the terrified prey of a murderous tyrannosaur was seen by some as a particularly meretricious instance of Spielberg's manipulation of the audience. A narrow view, it would seem. The device of placing the most vulnerable in the greatest peril is a basic component of cinematic suspense, and the introduction of the young and innocent to unspeakable terror a perfectly legitimate ploy and not out of place in a children's context. Spielberg as a child would have wept as most did, this writer included, when Bambi was orphaned by the deer hunters.

The public response to *Jurassic Park* was astounding. In the United States it swept ahead to reach an eventual gross of $357 million, and worldwide it powered on to reach a combined total of $913 million, soaring past *ET The Extra-Terrestrial*. In many countries the terms under which theatres were allowed to play it were onerous, but they did not deflect its appeal. There was an equivalent sum earned in respect of the spin-offs, the toys, models, books and other *Jurassic Park*-derived items. Allegedly Spielberg eventually made $250 million from his film, thanks to a generous points deal factored by Mike Ovitz. It is still the largest sum any individual has ever made from one movie.

18 Survival

The Earth-moving commercial success of *Jurassic Park* was all the more remarkable for the fact that throughout the shoot Spielberg was actively engaged in pre-production of his next film, and then actually left the editing for two weeks in order to start shooting it in Poland. With George Lucas as his *Jurassic Park* supervisor, he rented two satellite channels through a Polish television station (for $1.5 million a week) and keeping them open all the time, had downloaded from Hollywood each day the visuals on one and the sound through the other. He would then spend his evenings and weekends working on them with video equipment. Sometimes the dedication of film-makers, however eminent and successful, is under-estimated, and Spielberg had assumed a workload that would have floored lesser men.

Even more remarkably there were no points of similarity between the two films. The novel, *Schindler's List*, an inspiring work by the Australian writer Thomas Kenneally, had been published in the United States in 1982, and is essentially a true story, the account of a wealthy member of the Nazi party who systematically rescued hundreds of Jews from the gas chambers. Kenneally had chosen to put it in the form of a novel in order to speculate on the ambiguities residing in the story. He wrote it, however, after extensively travelling to visit the sites and to interview nearly fifty of the survivors who owed their lives to Oskar Schindler. In Britain his book was called *Schindler's Ark*, although to reduce confusion the publishers reverted to the American title after the film's release. As early as its initial publication Universal had earmarked it as a possible Spielberg project on his insistence, which was a prescient decision on their part in that his big film that year was the very different *ET*, and a grim story of the Holocaust could hardly have seemed the most appropriate material for him to pursue. Given Spielberg's unprecedented command of the box office it is likely that any of his suggestions would have been taken seriously.

Nevertheless, he realized that he was unready to go ahead with it, and that he would need to find considerable maturity as a film-maker first if he was to meet the emotional challenge that it involved. In 1983 he told the first Schindler survivor that he met that he would not make the film for ten years. It was an entirely accurate forecast. During the intervening decade he was to give the project constant thought. On more than one occasion he urged the Polish-born director Roman Polanski to take it up. Polanski had seen his parents seized by the Nazis, and his mother had perished in the Auschwitz gas chambers. A child at the time, he had escaped from the ghetto before the application of the Final Solution, and lived by his wits for the rest of the war, even at one time finding that he was the object of target practice by German soldiers. He was not particularly anxious to reopen his terrible memories. Spielberg had asked Kenneally to write a screenplay but was not too happy with it, and approached other writers. Martin Scorsese was then urged to direct, with Spielberg producing, and it was his idea to commission a script from Steven Zaillian. Then Spielberg changed his mind, deciding he wanted to direct it himself, and so swapped *Schindler's List* for the remake of *Cape Fear* which he had been thinking of directing. *Schindler's List* reverted to Spielberg and Scorsese took over *Cape Fear*, which he made for Amblin in 1992.

Another director who had expressed an interest was Billy Wilder, an Austrian Jew who had begun his film career at the Ufa studios in Berlin in the dying days of the Weimar republic and had then left Germany to avoid the Nazis, eventually reaching Hollywood at the invitation of his already installed compatriot, Joe May. Understandably Wilder had wanted to conclude his long career with a more distinguished film than the Lemmon–Matthau comedy *Buddy, Buddy*, and even now, in his mid-nineties, still has hopes of doing so, going to his office off Rodeo Drive every day to see what is happening, although it is no longer *Schindler's List* that he has his eye on. He was to offer Spielberg generous and deep-felt praise when he saw the finished film, having lost many of his own relations at Auschwitz.

The momentum to make the film gathered as Spielberg became aware of the effects of 'ethnic cleansing' in Bosnia and that death camps were yet again to be found in Europe. There were growing numbers of ultra-right revisionists who denied the Holocaust altogether or argued that its effects had been greatly exaggerated, and who were able to pass on their views to the gullible and ignorant. New generations, born long after the events in question, had very little idea of the history of the 1930s and 1940s. Researchers have found that a considerable proportion of young people of college age do not know who Roosevelt and Churchill were or even which sides they were on, and do not regard it as having any importance. It is hard, however, to be a Jew and not feel an atavistic sense of pain from the Holocaust. Spielberg, whose upbringing had not been religiously strict, began to examine his faith. There had never been any reason before why he should have made the fact that he was a Jew relevant to his work, and his films had been designed for universal appeal, regardless of beliefs. That was now to change.

The character of Oskar Schindler seemed to him to be extraordinary, a paradoxical figure. Superficially an opportunistic businessman, he could exercise superhuman powers of subterfuge, regardless of personal risk. Spielberg recognized in him some of the traits, especially the manipulative charm, of his friend and mentor Steve Ross, who was dying of cancer as the film was in preparation. He even showed home movies of Ross to Liam Neeson, the actor he selected to play Schindler, and instructed him to watch and be prepared to copy some of the mannerisms.

Schindler did not conform to the heroic stereotype. He was fallible, a hard-living gambler, a boozing womanizer and a ruthless business operator. He treated his wife appallingly and generally behaved like a blackguard. He had joined the Nazis mainly in order to make money from them, attending numerous social functions in order to butter up high-placed contacts in the hope of securing profitable deals. At the start of the war he went to Poland with the intention of using Jewish labour at starvation rates to work his factory, and so become a war-created tycoon. Yet at some point during the war there was an astounding transformation, a realization of the evil that was being perpetrated against fellow Europeans, and in spite of the profound difference it made to his entire outlook, he was able to conceal it from his Nazi paymasters. In one act of astounding bravado he even went after a train in which some of his women workers had been transported to Auschwitz, and secured an agreement to allow them to be released so that they could return to their allegedly essential war work, which actually consisted of making kitchen utensils. Having seen that the camp commandant had been adequately rewarded, he was able to spirit the wretched people away to protected safety. Schindler practised a series of audacious deceptions on the Germans and never raised their suspicions. There are thousands of Jews alive today who are the descendants of Schindler's Jews, their existence owed to one man who achieved more than governments in stemming a portion of the genocide against their race.

It is possible that Spielberg recognized in him a kindred spirit. They both had masks to wear. Schindler's public image turned out to be very different from the inner man. In Spielberg's case the creator of hugely successful moneymaking films that netted him personal wealth almost beyond comprehension concealed a strong social conscience, and a desire to do good. At large it was perceived as a curious project for him, and something of an indulgence on the part of Universal to allow him the budget which, as it happened, was relatively low for a Spielberg film, around $23 million. The hope was that it would break even, but it certainly was not expected to make money. Spielberg had generated so much income for the industry in his time that a little latitude was not out of place. That he was tackling the controversial and difficult subject of the Holocaust certainly evoked respect from the large Hollywood Jewish community.

He prepared by watching several times over Claude Lanzmann's remarkable nine-and-a-half-hour documentary *Shoah*, which tells the story of the Holocaust without using any archive footage, instead subjecting those who were party to it to a relentless inquisition, and allowing some of the survivors to describe their torments, and by letting the camera inspect the now-tranquil scenes of the horror. It is a deeply affecting work, but Spielberg discerned that the approach he would take would complement rather than supersede it. There were a few cynics who suggested that the only reason Spielberg was making his film was as a blatant attempt at Oscar-chasing. He responded with an anguished rebuttal.

The film was to be made entirely on location, and in black-and-white, much of it shot with a handheld camera. Janusz Kaminski, a Pole who had worked in Hollywood, was to be the cinematographer. The production designer, Allan Starski, was also Polish, and the line producer, Branko Lustig, was an actual child survivor of Auschwitz. In Kraków Spielberg was able to use Schindler's apartment building and factory among other sites that had been part of the reality. Unfortunately the World Jewish Congress, apprehensive of an influx of Hollywood-style extras, withheld permission for him to film within the walls of Auschwitz, so Spielberg built a concentration camp set outside the elaborate gatehouse through which the railway tracks passed, and the effect was chillingly real. Starski also had to build the Plaszów camp near the real location which had changed too much since 1945.

Spurning the starry possibilities of Harrison Ford, Kevin Costner and Mel Gibson as Schindler, Spielberg selected the Northern Irish actor Liam Neeson, having seen him on Broadway in a revival of Eugene O'Neill's *Anna Christie*, and deciding that his large, rugged physical presence seemed to conceal a deep-seated tender compassion. Neeson's career had run unevenly, but at the time of his performance as the seaman Matt Burke, opposite Natasha Richardson, who shortly afterwards became his wife, he was on masterly form. The next key character was that of Itzhak Stern, Schindler's Jewish accountant and business manager who was an amalgam of several employees, an invention of the screenwriter Steven Zaillian to serve as his conscience. He knows that by holding on to his job, which means exercising maximum efficiency, he can survive, but far from toadying to his boss it is almost the other way round, with Schindler seemingly keen to stay in favour. Stern is the means by which Schindler can carry out his plan, and it is he who makes the selection of the people who are to be saved. They never discuss its outcome; there is simply a tacit understanding between them on what

The Academy finally acknowledged Spielberg for Schindler's List. **The film won seven awards, including best picture and best director. In his acceptance speech he said, 'If I hadn't gotten it, I would have been shattered.'**

they are doing. The Anglo-Indian actor Ben Kingsley, who had won the best actor Oscar for his performance as Gandhi in Richard Attenborough's 1982 film biography, was cast in the role and proved to be an admirable choice in spite of his not being Jewish. (Earlier he had appeared as the gangster Meyer Lansky in Warren Beatty's *Bugsy*, a very different kind of Jew.) The third key role was that of Amon Goeth, the commandant of Plaszów, with whom Schindler must deal, an individual steeped in demonic malevolence, but far from the clichéd Nazi types that Hollywood usually places in charge of prison camps. Another British actor, Ralph Fiennes, fitted the part, Spielberg noting after his screen test that he could turn on a positively sexual evil at will. 'There were moments of kindness that would move across his eyes. Then they'd instantly turn cold.' He was to play a man who would amuse himself in the mornings, while he was shaving, by picking off inmates from his balcony and shooting them dead.

Making the film was a harrowing experience, leaving mental scars on everyone involved. The extras were recruited locally and carefully chosen, because they had to appear under-nourished. They were to undergo an appalling ordeal, having, for instance, to be stripped naked and made to run in front of German doctors as they make the choice between those who would be spared for labour, and those who would go to the gas chambers. 'Every day,' said Spielberg, 'was like waking up and going to hell.' Keeping him mentally intact was the presence in Poland of his wife and children, and on a couple of desperate occasions he telephoned his friend Robin Williams and persuaded him to do twenty minutes of his most zany *schtick* so that he could have a laugh for the first time in many weeks.

Some sequences make for hard viewing. The liquidation of the Kraków ghetto, mostly shot with handheld cameras, takes up over a quarter of an hour of running time, and maintains its intensity throughout, as troops pour in, invading each dwelling, shooting those who try to resist, wrenching children from their mothers, and thrusting those destined for the camps into trucks. Some of the victims try to conceal their valuables; others attempt to squeeze into hiding places, but are rooted out with chilling efficiency, the searchers using stethoscopes to detect signs of breathing behind the plaster. A small boy even jumps into a nauseous, brimming cesspit to avoid discovery. Schindler has gone riding that day with his mistress, and watches the terrible scenes from an overlooking hill. In one of the very few camera tricks used in the film, catching his eye is a little girl in a dingy red coat, and she turns up again, the same smudge of colour, much later in a pile of corpses.

It is not the only time that colour is used in this lengthy black-and-white film. At the beginning a family prays for the Sabbath, and lights the candles, which burn down in a series of dissolves. The film ends with a present-day epilogue in the Catholic cemetery on Mount Zion, Jerusalem, in which more than a hundred of Schindler's Jews and their kin, and actors in the film, file past his grave, each depositing a stone on it in accordance with custom. It was thought that even Spielberg himself is briefly glimpsed, but it has been denied. That Schindler is buried in Jerusalem is a particular honour. He died in 1974, after a difficult career in which several business ventures failed. He was sustained by money donated by the survivors in gratitude. In the film, as the magnitude of his deed sinks in, his workers remove their gold fillings, which were usually left intact by the Nazis until they had become corpses, and melt them down to make a ring for their benefactor. Spielberg was given a replica of the real ring by the survivors, and found within its circle the inscription 'You save one life, you save the world.' He had copies made to be presented to Lew Wasserman and Sid Sheinberg, the two of the Universal top brass who had helped his career the most.

The film opened in the United States in early December 1993 in time to qualify for the Academy Awards, and far enough ahead of Christmas not to collide with the more festive fare that Hollywood was offering. The critical response was overwhelmingly favourable, the one area of dissent oddly being that of the Jewish press, which concluded that it disliked the Holocaust being turned into a background for fiction. The film was not a documentary but an interpretation of Kenneally's novel, which had already taken a few liberties with the truth. For instance, Schindler in the film secures the release of the women prisoners dispatched by train to Auschwitz after a few hours of hard bargaining, during which time they have been sent naked into the showers where they expect to be gassed. It actually took him three weeks to free them.

It would seem that the pain evoked by the subject matter was impossible to encompass. Spielberg was particularly upset to find that Claude Lanzmann, the director of the documentary *Shoah* which he had admired, resolving not to intrude on its approach to the subject, dismissed *Schindler's List* out of hand, condemning it as work of fiction. Spielberg responded by accusing Lanzmann of wanting to be 'the only voice in the definitive document of the Holocaust', and went on to say that he was amazed that there 'could be any hurt feelings in an effort to reflect the truth'.

Spielberg was acting as a popularizer, working in a popular medium. To a large percentage of the non-Jewish filmgoing public the Holocaust, if they had even heard of it, occurred so many years before they were born that it had as much relevance as the American Civil War or the Great Fire of London. Spielberg was applying a corrective, a remedial course in learning of a dreadful episode of twentieth-century history. The box-office response completely defied the forecasts, and the film's eventual worldwide gross was to be $321 million, $96 million of which was earned in US domestic rentals, an unusual balance reflecting that it was received more enthusiastically in other countries. Universal had hardly expected it to reach break-even point, let alone become one of the top hits of the year. Free screenings were laid on for students, and it received a presidential endorsement from Bill Clinton. In Germany special efforts were made for young people to see it and acquire some knowledge of a past that their grandparents would have known.

The public awareness of the Spielbergian feel-good factor over the years was still a handicap. Although he won another DGA award, he had the chagrin of the Los Angeles and New York critics selecting it as the best film of the year, and then failing to name him as best director. The Academy, however, gave it eleven nominations. On Oscar night it received seven awards. Neeson and Fiennes were unsuccessful, but Steven Zaillian was honoured for the screenplay, Allan Starski for the production design, Janusz Kaminski for cinematography, Michael Kahn for editing and John Williams for the score. Gratifyingly, it was not only named as the best picture, with Spielberg, Gerald R. Molen and Branko Lustig, the three producers, receiving the award, but there was also an Oscar for best director. Said Spielberg in his acceptance speech, relishing the fact that at last, after so many rebuffs, he was standing on the podium and receiving the coveted award: 'If I hadn't gotten it, I would have been shattered.'

19 Return of the Monsters

His awakened conscience prompted Spielberg to adopt a more public position with regard to his Jewish heritage. He founded the Righteous Persons Foundation, dedicating it to the memory of Schindler, with the purpose of commemorating those Gentiles who had rescued Jews from the Holocaust. It has funded both individuals – artists, writers, documentary film-makers – and Jewish charities, and has helped in the restoration of the Anne Frank House in Amsterdam, a memorial visited by many thousands of tourists each year. Spielberg also founded the Survivors of Shoah Visual History Foundation, which took on as its task the recording of first-hand accounts from the remaining survivors, a mammoth undertaking which has to be accomplished as quickly as possible while they are still alive. The funding, from the profits of *Schindler's List*, was augmented by contributions from Time-Warner, NBC, MCA and the Lew Wasserman Foundation, all of which had been involved in Spielberg projects. Using multimedia techniques on a prodigious scale, the archive is intended to be the most comprehensive record ever assembled on the Holocaust, a permanent source of information for scholars and an ultimate, shaming rebuttal to those who claim that it never happened, or has been greatly exaggerated.

Following the release of *Jurassic Park* and *Schindler's List* over so short a period Spielberg felt that it was an appropriate time to take a sabbatical from directing, a decision that was widely proclaimed in the media. It did not, however, mean that he was temporarily quitting the business altogether. The Hollywood power structure was undergoing upheaval. Mike Ovitz had become the most important agent, with stars such as Redford, Hoffman, Connery, Streisand, de Niro, Costner, Stallone and Cruise appearing on his client list, as well as the film-makers Scorsese, Coppola, Stone, Levinson, Burton and Spielberg. He had achieved enormous domination in the industry from his ability to broker package deals at monumental prices, and had become feared and loathed in many quarters. One of the anti-Ovitz contingent was David Geffen, whose meteoric ascent had been through the record business, where he had accomplished a few masterstroke deals that had made him richer even than Spielberg. Another was Jeffrey Katzenberg, the awesomely capable president of production at Disney who had propelled *The Lion King* into becoming the most profitable animated feature of all time. He had coveted the position held by Frank Wells, the Disney president and CEO, who was killed in a helicopter crash in April 1994, but Michael Eisner, the chairman hesitated, then imported Joe Roth from Twentieth Century Fox to share the job with Katzenberg, who soon resigned in dudgeon. He was already a partner with Spielberg in a fast-food submarine-sandwich chain called Dive!, which carried the theme-park approach to eating, with spectacular side effects as the entire place at regular intervals prepared to submerge.

A gargantuan partnership of titans, a 'dream team', came into being. DreamWorks SKG – the initials standing for Spielberg, Katzenberg and Geffen – was the biggest challenge to the spread of Ovitz's octopoid reach, and the biggest studio launch since the formation of Twentieth Century Fox sixty years earlier. Its ambitions were enormous, a new studio together with a housing development and marina on 1,100 acres at Playa Vista, where Howard Hughes had built his ill-fated flying-boat, the *Spruce Goose*, an animation centre in Glendale and a commitment to new technology leading to participation by Microsoft. Such was the confidence of the leading players that they reinvented arithmetic by investing $100 million in exchange for two-thirds of the company, the remaining $900 raised from elsewhere resulting in a one-third ownership. DreamWorks will take time to bring rewards to its backers, and the early films such as the thriller *The Peacemaker*, a box-office lemon, suggest that early days are still here, and the best, it is to be hoped, is yet to come. The Playa Vista development has been bogged down in environmental arguments over the importance of the wetlands that the complex would displace, and some operations, such as the interactive film division, have now been wound up. In September 1997 the *New York Times* commented scathingly that DreamWorks had managed to get through $1 billion of the $2.7 billion for which the company was capitalized, with precious little to show for it.

When Spielberg resumed directing it was perhaps disappointing that having moved so far into a more weighty kind of film with *Schindler's List* he then regressed to his old commercially minded self to make the sequel to the film that had preceded it. Arguably, whatever he made after *Schindler's List* would be something of an anticlimax, and in any case, having gone through the longest period of his career without directing a feature himself (he had been busy executive-producing items as varied as *The Flintstones*, *Casper*, *The Bridges of Madison County*, *How to Make an American Quilt*, *Balto*, *Twister* and *Men in Black*, a mixed bag ranging from the dire to the ultra-successful) he would have to ease himself back into directing carefully.

Eventually his new film was to take as its title the somewhat clumsy form of punctuation-lacking wording, *The Lost World Jurassic Park*. It was a blatant allusion to the Conan Doyle fantasy novel that had been filmed in 1925 as a silent directed by Harry Hoyt, with its monsters created by Willis O'Brien, who was to make a rather better job of it with *King Kong* a few years later. *The Lost World* had been remade in CinemaScope in 1960, as an undistinguished film directed by Irwin Allen, and more recently there was a Canadian production, directed by Timothy Bond in 1993. The title was not the only second-hand aspect to Spielberg's new work, which had been written by David Koepp from Michael Crichton's novel. The logo was almost identical to that of Spielberg's original film, although the dinosaur silhouette was somewhat more wasted in appearance, and, as so often happens with sequels, several elements in the story coincided almost exactly. But then, as we have already seen, the story was not the strong point of the original film, either.

The opening sequence fulfilled the purpose of filling the audience with anxiety, as a wealthy family picnics by the sandy shore of an idyllic tropical isle. The ominous John Williams score indicates that all may not be well, as a child wanders out of sight. There is a commotion, running, terror. A little girl has been attacked by tiny, bird-like dinosaurs called compsognathusi that have somehow broken loose from a breeding site on the island which lies adjacent to the one on which all the trouble happened before. Here the animals have been allowed to live as naturally as possible, within their own ecosystem, which has allowed them to be self-supporting. The ending of the first film, as the survivors leave the main island, clearly indicated that a sequel was a predictable option. The new scenario is that after the destruction left behind then, InGen, the company founded by John Hammond (Richard Attenborough again, but older, wearier and without his earlier Scottish accent), has a new board headed by his nephew (Arliss Howard). Jeff Goldblum has also survived from the first film, and he is asked to return to make a scientific survey, and he swallows his reluctance because his paleontologist girlfriend (Julianne Moore) is already there. 'Don't worry,' says Hammond. 'I'm not going to make the same mistakes again.' 'No,' says Goldblum, still playing the cynic, 'you're making new ones.'

Accompanied by a video director (Vince Vaughn) and an equipment specialist, as well as his doughty, acrobatic teenage daughter (Vanessa Lee Chester), who has inveigled her way into the party, Goldblum reaches the island, but the new chief executive arrives with an eager hunter (Pete Postlethwaite) intending to catch his prey to ship back to San Diego where a new Jurassic Park will be sited on the American

At the American Jewish Awards in 1997. Following Schindler's
List**, Spielberg decided to adopt a more public position with
regard to his Jewish heritage.**

mainland. The video-maker is against the idea and frees them, but the compsognathusi stampede and, in a spectacular sequence, push the vehicle containing all the surveillance equipment over a cliff, leading to a hair-raising escape as it teeters over a sheer drop. Trekking back to base the party is attacked by velociraptors and in an amazing overhead shot as they make their way through long grass the trails of the creatures are seen converging on them.

To pursue Conan Doyle's story further, a fully grown tyrannosaur is taken to California and breaks loose, creating mayhem through San Diego. King Kong rampaging through New York is as nothing compared with the way this beast chews up the comfortable white-collar neighbourhoods that are so similar to those in *ET* and *Poltergeist*. Yet the Godzilla-like urban trashing comes almost as a postscript to the rest of the film, and although the CGI spectacle is superbly realized, it adds little in originality.

In the four-year interim between the two films computer techniques had advanced rapidly and Spielberg's film served as a showcase for the electronic special-effects experts. Budgeted at $73 million, with locations ranging from Queensland to New Zealand and Hawaii to California, it was intended to be a big blockbuster film. It was also darker in tone than the first *Jurassic Park*, with seemingly a far higher body count. The incident of the little girl at the beginning would have been enough to have given parents worries that it was not really family fare, and the *Washington Post* concluded its review with the strange admonition: 'PG–13 – Scenes of human carnage may scare small children and intellectuals.' It was not too well regarded by critics, who felt that little new dramatic ground was covered. Nevertheless, its box-office performance was outstanding, achieving $93 million on its opening weekend and a domestic gross of $229 million, plus a further $382 million in the rest of the world.

20 Liberty Triumphs

In 1984 the versatile actress-dancer Debbie Allen discovered, by reading two volumes of essays, an incident in the history of black America that had previously eluded her. The subject under discussion was a mutiny on board a Spanish slave ship called *La Amistad* that occurred in 1839. She was so taken with the implications of the affair that she optioned a book recounting the affair, *Black Mutiny: The Revolt on the Schooner Amistad* by William A. Owens, and resolved that she would eventually bring it to the screen. In attempting to sell the idea she experienced a total lack of interest, and the years passed. When in 1993 she saw *Schindler's List* it occurred to her that there was possibility that Steven Spielberg might be persuaded. The thought was prescient. Two of the seven children in the extended Spielberg family, Theo and Mikaela George, are adopted African-Americans, and having made *The Color Purple* his sympathies for American blacks were openly accountable. A meeting with him was set up by DreamWorks executives. It turned out to be a propitious occasion. Spielberg relentlessly questioned Debbie Allen and seemed to share her fascination for the story. He, too, had barely heard of it, and lapped up the details from her. She later described the meeting, saying that she had the feeling that he felt it was a story that he should be able to pass on to his children. It would become the first film he was to direct for DreamWorks.

The ship, having left Sierra Leone with fifty-three African men who had been forcibly seized and removed from their families, had crossed the Atlantic and was off the coast of Cuba when the captives crammed and shackled below decks managed to break loose and take control of it. Their intention was to turn about and sail back home but, lacking navigational skills, they were forced to rely on the only two crew members who were left on board, the others having been killed in the struggle or put ashore. They were deceived, and after several weeks were off the coast of Long Island at Montauk. There they were taken prisoner by the American navy, and charged with piracy and murder, both capital offences. There were considerable political implications. The abolitionists immediately saw a cause to champion, but Martin Van Buren, the eighth president of the United States, although a New Yorker, was anxious not to lose precious votes in the southern, slave-owning states in the forthcoming election of 1840, and also had no wish to upset Spain and the young Queen Isabella, who was baying for blood. The prisoners were her property, she claimed, and must be returned to Spain. There were attempts from this high level to manipulate the subsequent trial in New Haven, Connecticut, and a favourable verdict for the accused was thrown out, and a retrial set with a more pliant judge. Eventually a former president, the lawyer and diplomat John Quincy Adams, was urged from retirement to defend the prisoners as the case went to the Supreme Court, which, in spite of its pro-slavery weighting, was swayed by his arguments, and with only one dissenting vote, freed the men.

The screenplay, inevitably compressing and eliding many aspects of the story, was written by David Franzoni, and is told from the perspective of the mutineers, who were led by an articulate and intelligent African called Sengbe Pieh, his name rendered in Spanish as Cinque. In the film he is played by Djimon Hounsou, a striking Beninese who had lived many years in Paris, and had been used as a model by the fashion designer Thierry Mughler. Spielberg's *Amistad* was his first starring film role. The distinguished black actor Morgan Freeman was cast as a fictitious abolitionist, formerly a slave himself, the character representing a number of emancipated black Americans who devoted their freedom to the cause of their enslaved brothers. Roger Baldwin, the young property lawyer with an indifferent reputation who becomes the defendants' advocate, is played by Matthew McConaughey. Initially he is sceptical, but as the case progresses he undergoes a transformation, eventually advancing ingenious arguments to establish his premise that his clients were illegally abducted in the first place and are exercising their natural rights.

By an interesting quirk of casting the roles of the two presidents were both taken by British actors. The wily, manipulative Van Buren is played by Nigel Hawthorne and the aged, sternly moral Adams by Anthony Hopkins, who had already played another American president as the leading character in Oliver Stone's *Nixon*. Sir Anthony, portraying an orator of distinction, has at the climax of the film a lengthy speech to deliver to the Supreme Court which draws on the Declaration of Independence, to which Adams's father, John Adams, was a signatory. The speech that in reality lasted for many hours and embraced a multitude of detailed legal arguments takes merely eleven minutes of screen time, and is mostly a stirring reminder of the thoughts on liberty that the founding fathers enshrined in the Declaration of Independence in 1776. Another Briton, Pete Postlethwaite, plays the prosecutor. David Paymer is Van Buren's secretary of state, and Anna Paquin plays the girl queen, Isabella of Spain. As a felicitous touch, the Supreme Court judge who pronounces the ultimate verdict of 1841 is a real former member of that bench, Justice Harry A. Blackmun. The Africans were recruited from the Mende tribe, whose language is spoken in the film, and from various countries of west Africa. One of the points emphasized in the film is the failure of communication between the defendants and the court, with nobody able to understand their obscure tribal tongue. For the Africans it was a long and arduous shoot, and the chains and shackles they wore were real, resulting in pain and discomfort as well as an inkling for both cast and crew of what it must have been like on the terrible ocean journey.

The creative team of *Amistad* was made up mostly from those who had worked with Spielberg on previous films. Janusz Kaminski, the cinematographer of *Schindler's List*, the production designer Rick Carter who had worked on both *Jurassic Park* films, with Michael Kahn, who had won Oscars for *Raiders of the Lost Ark* and *Schindler's List*, as editor, and John Williams, a veteran of countless Spielberg films, was responsible for the score. A director is always much more at ease if all his department heads are familiar with him and his way of working. Standing in for New Haven more than a century and a half ago a section of Newport, Rhode Island, with characteristic buildings of the period was used. Tons of earth spread across the street and the removal of modern lighting columns and parking meters restored the mid-nineteenth-century appearance. Mystic Seaport, a working maritime museum in Connecticut, provided nautical locations, and the domed Massachusetts State House in Boston stood in for the House of Representatives. At the time of the *Amistad* affair the Capitol dome was still nearly twenty years from completion, so an anachronism resulted. Washington refused permission for the Supreme Court to be used and it was recreated on a sound stage. The most impressive outdoor construction was the prison, a stern, stone fortress which was built in the middle of Newport, its grim architecture in total contrast with the elegant New England-style surrounding buildings. The studio-assembled interior was equally forbidding, a dark, desolate place of confinement, heaving with the bodies of the incarcerated Africans, with little more space at the disposal than they had on their hated slave ship.

As so often happens when film-makers turn to historical subjects Spielberg found that he had entered a minefield laid by academics with regard to the accuracy of his treatment of the story. Some of the criticisms were quibbles. The relationship between Cinque and Adams did not include a meeting at home, a key scene in the film in which the two men whose backgrounds could hardly have been further apart establish a philosophical rapport. Some historians believe that on his return to Africa Cinque became a slave-trader himself, an outcome that would seriously inconvenience Spielberg's desire to elevate him to a noble stature. Spielberg does make the point that much of the slave trade was in the hands of Africans, who ran a

Sir Anthony Hopkins played the sternly moral John Quincy Adams in Amistad.

notorious slave fort in Sierra Leone. He was criticized for pandering to chic liberalism in suggesting that black Africa and white Europe were on level pegging in civilization terms, which was the case two millennia earlier but did not prevail in the nineteenth century. A lengthy article in the *New Yorker* by Simon Schama, demolishing Spielberg's elementary history lesson, amounted to a severe academic rubbishing.

The problem with all films that deal with real events is that in order to dramatize them for the screen, and to make them comprehensible to audiences within the running time, many compromises have to be made for the sake of the unity of performance. The dramatic film-maker is not a documentary director, but an impressionist. Griffith, who even somewhat tediously cited historical sources on inter-titles for *The Birth of a Nation*, made many presumptions that distorted the truth. Eisenstein created the indelible images of the massacre on the Odessa Steps in *Battleship Potemkin* and the storming of the Winter Palace in *October* and even though they never happened that way they have found their way into popular perceptions of revolutionary Russia. David Lean's compelling portrayal of T. E. Lawrence in *Lawrence of Arabia* is an astonishing fictionalization of history, not least for the fact that his small, slender hero was played by a man well over six feet tall. None of this detracts from the integrity of the films in question.

At the root of *Amistad* is Spielberg's belief in tolerance and the will enshrined within the Declaration of Independence to embrace the ideal of guaranteed freedom. At the time of *Amistad* its implementation had a distance to go, and for that reason the case is a milestone on the route towards the Civil War twenty years later. Using considerable dramatic licence, he made it symbolic of a struggle that continues to this day, mindful that in Los Angeles the authorities are constantly uncovering sweatshops where illegal immigrants have been shipped in to work on starvation wages. In the New Haven courtroom as the legal deliberations grind on, one acquittal having been overturned on presidential intervention, together with the appointment of a new judge who is expected to be more compliant, Cinque, with his minimal grasp of English, utters the cry 'Give us free', which is then taken up by the other defendants who chant it over and over, the officers unable to stop them. 'Give us free' is the essence of what Spielberg's film is all about.

It is remarkable that the British, so frequently portrayed in Hollywood films as arrogant white supremacists, are actually accorded a favourable role for once, with an officer of the Royal Navy attesting as a witness against the entire ethos of slavery. It was a justifiable position, since Great Britain was the second European country (after Denmark) to abolish the trade, in 1807, and passed an emancipation bill in 1825. After the *Amistad* case Britain and America jointly undertook to stop the illegal transportation, and in the final moments of the Spielberg film a British warship bombards the African slave fort, releasing its inmates who have been seized and herded to await a ship for North America.

An attack on the moral stance of the film was one thing, but Spielberg had to face another, potentially dangerous broadside in the form of a $10 million plagiarism suit filed by the black writer Barbara Chase-Riboud, who claimed that her book *Echo of Lions* had been shamelessly lifted. Such accusations are frequent within the film industry, and simultaneously Spielberg was defending himself against another writer who alleged that *Twister*, a film that he produced, had used an idea lock, stock and barrel from a script submitted some time before it went into production. Chase-Riboud claimed that her book had been submitted to Amblin in 1988 by Jacqueline Kennedy Onassis, who was then working for a New York publisher. At the time it was rejected for filming, although it was not returned. Some six years later it was optioned by Dustin Hoffman, who commissioned a screenplay by David Franzoni. It went unfilmed. Franzoni was also Spielberg's screenwriter for the DreamWorks production of *Amistad*, which was completed without reference to Chase-Riboud's book. The only literary source referred to in the screen credits is the account by William A. Owens, *Black Mutiny: The Revolt on the Schooner Amistad* which Debbie Allen had initially brought to Spielberg when he first became interested in the idea. The end credits also carry acknowledgements to eleven academics and a number of historic institutions. It is difficult in the case of a book based on true-life incidents to establish a copyright since the events themselves are in the public domain, and anyone can go to the same source material. Chase-Riboud claimed to have identified forty overwhelming similarities, and demanded a court injunction that would have prevented the film from opening. It was refused, with judgement reserved. Later she pronounced herself satisfied with the film itself, and the case appears settled.

The controversies in part detracted from the film's performance. In the winter of 1997–98 *Amistad* was, in the company of every other film that opened in the period, totally eclipsed by the runaway success of *Titanic*, and by the time of its opening in Britain at the end of February 1998 had only grossed $40 million in the United States, a figure roughly the same as its budget. James Cameron's film had meanwhile become the third most successful American release of all time, and was looking to be the first to crash through a worldwide gross of a billion dollars.

By the time of *Amistad*'s release Spielberg had finished shooting his next film, the production based in England, set in Europe during World War II before and after D-Day, with a spectacular re-creation of the battle for the Normandy beaches. For release in the summer of 1998, *Saving Private Ryan* stars Tom Hanks, who won the best actor Academy Award twice in succession for *Philadelphia* and *Forrest Gump*. The GI in the title is played by Matt Damon, who has been injured behind the German lines, and is rescued by a mission led by Hanks, a captain. The sergeant, who is second-in-command, is played by Tom Sizemore. Others in the company are Edward Burns, who is the streetwise New Yorker Reiben, the cynic in the group, Adam Goldberg and Van Diesel. The rescue of Ryan is primarily a propaganda exercise. He is the only one of four serving brothers still left alive, and the saving of his life is regarded as important not only for the morale of the army, but for the families of servicemen back in the United States.

Spielberg's inspiration was the true sacrifice of an American family, the Sullivans. In 1943 five brothers serving on the same ship died when it was sunk in battle with the Japanese. Shortly afterwards three of four brothers from another family were killed, and a search party was sent to locate the fourth, in order that he could be sent home. The war department soon put into effect an order preventing siblings from serving in the same fighting unit.

Much of *Saving Private Ryan* was shot on a disused British Aerospace airfield at Hatfield, near London, where there were large empty hangars that could be pressed into use as stages. A sizeable proportion of the $65

million budget went on the twenty-three-minute D-Day sequence which, owing to the lack, in England, of suitable beaches and the numbers of military extras needed, was shot in County Wexford, Eire, using soldiers from the Irish army. The cinematographer was Janusz Kaminski, who was responsible for *Schindler's List*.

By early 1998 Spielberg was fifty-one, although when interviewed at that time on BBC televison by my old friend and colleague Barry Norman, who spoke of him as having just turned fifty, he did not attempt to correct him. Perhaps if he had he would have found Dennis Hoffman emerging from the past to demand the honouring of his contract. He did, however, say that he had many more films to make, some of them serious, others as sheer entertainment, and that a fourth *Indiana Jones* film was looming in the imminent future. Such a gadfly approach to the movie business makes sense, and he would not be the first film-maker to finance his more worthy projects with crowd-pleasing hits. Given that he is now a studio boss as well, and the creative centre of DreamWorks, which still has to prove itself but has the potential to be a pacesetting force in the Hollywood of the twenty-first century, Spielberg will be around to delight his public for years to come.

DUEL

Wednesday, November 17, 1971

(Movie of the Weekend)

With Dennis Weaver, Eddie Firestone, Charles Seel, Lucille Benson, Tim Herbert, Alexander Lockwood, Amy Douglas, Gene Dynarski. Producer: George Eckstein. Director: Steven Spielberg. Writer: Richard Matheson. 90 Mins., Sat., 8:30 p.m. ABC-TV

In America, a man's car is his castle – a home away from home in which he is master of all he surveys. Put the average man, beset though he may be by a rotten boss, a nagging wife, whining kids and an insupportable mortgage, and his worries fall away. Speeding along the rolling highway with his fingertip controls and no lights along the way, 'Mr.' Average American becomes King Driver the First.

What happens then, when his fiefdom is attacked by another pretender to the throne. How well does this freeway monarch behave when his rolling fortress is besieged by an apparently stronger force.

This was the problem the Universal made-for-tv film wrestled with. Dennis Weaver played a salesman on his way to an appointment. He drove along a narrow highway located in a sparsely settled western locale. Along the way he passed an enormous oil tanker rig, and later he passed it again.

But, apparently this was the wrong thing to do. For the rig driver is not only also a king, but a tyrant to boot. From then on the picture was all chase–with the trucker alternately playing dangerous games with Weaver and then actually seeming to want to kill him. A clear case of absolute power corrupting absolutely.

Neither Weaver nor the tv audience ever got to see the face of the driver (indeed, he had no credit listing), beyond one view of his lower legs and feet and one of his hands waving Weaver on. At one point, Weaver got driven off the road.

Fortunately, it happened near a cafe and the shaken man got out to calm down. Instead he almost had a nervous breakdown and got beaten up when he accused another customer of being his assailant.

But once back in the car, Weaver (who believed his nemesis far along the road) relaxed and thought that, after all, it's a pretty nice day to be out driving. In fact, despite all the trouble and danger he encountered behind the wheel, Weaver was much more a whole man when driving than when afoot. And finally it was the car itself which became the instrument of his salvation – willing, it would seem, to be a sacrifice for its master. Ask the man who owns one if they still build them that way any more.

The story was adapted from a short tale in Playboy magazine. But it really played much more like one of those old dramas in the Golden Age of Radio.

For the most part, the production, although clearly not expensively mounted, kept within the spirit of the teleplay and helped it roll. One intrusive note was the necessity for a good deal of inner dialog voiced over the action to indicate Weaver's feelings.

Upfront, the show was gimmicky and full of logical holes. But at the end of the 90 minutes, it seemed to have taken no time at all – that's the way to run a highway.

Fob.

THE SUGARLAND EXPRESS

Wednesday, March 20, 1974

Goldie Hawn in hilarious chase comedy which turns sour in overkill climax.

Hollywood, Feb 27. Universal Pictures release. Produced by Richard D. Zanuck and David Brown. Stars Goldie Hawn. Directed by Steven Spielberg. Screenplay, Hal Barwood, Matthew Robbins, from a story by Spielberg, Barwood and Robbins; camera (Technicolor), Vilmos Zsigmond; editors, Edward M. Abroms, Verna Fields; music, John Williams; art direction, Joseph Alves Jr.; sound, John Carter, Robert Hovt; asst. director, James Fargo. Reviewed at Bruin Theatre, L.A., Feb. 26, '74. (MPAA Rating: PG.) Running time: 109 Mins. (Color)

Lou Jean Poplin	Goldie Hawn
Captain Tanner	Ben Johnson
Officer Slide	Michael Sacks
Clovis Poplin	William Atherton
Officer Mashburn	Gregory Walcott
Baby Langston	Harrison Zanuck

"The Sugarland Express" begins and plays for much of its length as a hilarious madcap caper chase comedy, a sort of live action, feature-length "Roadrunner" cartoon. Goldie Hawn stars as a young mother who helps husband William Atherton escape from prison so they may rescue their baby from involuntary adoption. Unfortunately, the film — having made in deft fashion its many telling points — degenerates in final reels to heavy-handed social polemic and sound-and-fury shootout, which leaves a sour taste in the heart. The technically handsome Richard D. Zanuck-David Brown production for Universal release, generally well directed by feature-debuting Steven Spielberg, should get off to a strong start although its legs could be wobbly.

Based on an actual event in Texas in 1969, the screenplay is by Hal Barwood and Matthew Robbins, from a story by them and Spielberg. Besides some excellent major characterizations — the couple, plus Michael Sacks as a patrol car officer whom they kidnap, and Ben Johnson, outstanding as a police captain who in effect becomes trail boss of a caravan of cop cars trailing the fugitives across the state — the comedic impact is enhanced by terrific visual staging. Carey Loftin staged the many action scenes and must in fairness share equal credit for the fun with the director and writers.

There's a built-in audience for the film — a large segment of the population that holds in amused contempt the tendency of today's hyper-mechanized police to swarm like bees around any event. Jaywalking busts often look no different from armed robbery arrests; flashing lights, radio calls, patrol cars akimbo on the roadway and sidewalk, doors askew — such is the busy work of today's law and order. Thus, as the film progresses, the police caravan grows and grows. Vilmos Zsigmond's versatile Panavision-Technicolor lensing catches all the inherent sight gags, including a hilarious poke at "eye-witness tv news" intrusions.

In counterpoint to the visual comedy, some fine character interplay develops between Hawn, Atherton and Sacks, and also between Johnson and his younger, trigger-happy zealots who would solve all problems with a bullet, preferably in the back, thus avoiding all that bother about perspective, evidence, justice, and other outdated concepts.

But then something happens to the picture. The light touch becomes heavy; the mood gets darker; instead of rapier thrusts, the filmmakers shift to crowbars and battle axes; the social commentary becomes frenzied, aimed lower towards the level of those playpen revolutionaries of the late '60s; despite the fact that the overhanging futility could have gradually segued into the plot, the story opts for an abrupt series of production number shootouts, as though this was the real purpose in making the film, and all that preceded was introductory filler and vamp. Too bad, for two-thirds of the film is artful, the rest strident.

Hawn's performance is generally delightful, despite her near-curtain screaming fit (occasionally confused with acting when such occurs). Atherton has the same likeable charisma that Keith Carradine no longer has a monopoly on. Sacks is excellent in shifting from one of those police academy automatons to a rounded human being. Johnson is just plain superb. The baby is son of the producer Richard Zanuck and wife Linda Harrison.

John Williams' score is very good, and Toots Thieleman's harmonica solos are an excellent highlight. Loftin and his logistics crew contributed outstanding work. At nearly 109 minutes, the film distends its welcome.

Murf.

JAWS

Wednesday, June 18, 1975

Excellent filmization of the book. Smash b.o. outlook.

Hollywood, April 25. Universal Pictures release, produced by Richard D. Zanuck, David Brown. Stars Roy Scheider, Robert Shaw, Richard Dreyfuss. Directed by Steven Spielberg. Screenplay, Peter Benchley, Carl Gottlieb, based on Benchley's novel; camera (Technicolor), Bill Butler; underwater camera, Rexford Metz; shark footage, Ron and Valerie Taylor; editor, Verna Fields; music, John Williams; production design, Joseph Alves Jr.; set decoration, John M Dwyer; sound, John R. Carter, Robert Hoyt; asst. director, Tom Joyner. Reviewed at Cinerama Dome Theatre, L.A., April 24, '75 (MPAA Rating: PG.) Running time, 124 Mins. (Color).

Chief Martin Brody	Roy Scheider
Quint	Robert Shaw
Matt Hooper	Richard Dreyfuss
Mrs. Brody	Lorraine Gary
Mayor Vaughn	Murray Hamilton
Editor Meadows	Carl Gottlieb
Policeman Hendricks	Jeffrey Kramer
Chrissie	Susan Backlinie
Cassidy	Jonathan Filley
Estuary Victim	Ted Grossman
Brody Children	Chris Rebello, Jay Mello
Mrs Kintner	Lee Fierro
Alex Kintner	Jeffrey Voorhees
Ben Gardner	Craig Kingsbury
Medical Examiner	Robert Nevin
TV newsman	Peter Benchley

Getting right to the point, "Jaws" is an artistic and commercial smash. Producers Richard D. Zanuck and David Brown, and director Steven Spielberg, have the satisfaction of a production problem-plagued film turning out beautifully. Peter Benchley's bestseller about a killer shark and a tourist beach town has become a film consummate suspense, tension and terror. The Universal release looks like a torrid money-maker everywhere.

Spielberg's feature debut last year in "The Sugarland Express" also a Zanuck/Brown pic, was greeted with a measure of critical ecstacy not echoed by the public; domestic film rentals on it were not even $3,100,000 after seven months in release. However, story considerations aside, Spielberg's directorial abilities on that one as well as "Jaws" display a remarkable grasp of both logistics and drama. The assured success of "Jaws" will minimize the 100% budget over-run, to the neighborhood of $8,000,000.

Author Benchley and Carl Gottlieb share adaptation credit for "Jaws," and the literate screenplay moves easily from large-scale mob scenes to extremely intimate situations. There are three stars: Roy Scheider, very effective as the town's police chief torn between civic duty and the mercantile politics of resort tourism; Robert Shaw, absolutely magnificent as a coarse fisherman finally hired to locate the Great White Shark; and Richard Dreyfuss, in another excellent characterization as a likeable young scientist.

The fast-moving 124-minute film engenders enormous suspense as the shark attacks a succession of people; the creature is not even seen for about 82 minutes, and a subjective camera technique makes his earlier forays excruciatingly terrifying all the more for the invisibility. The final hour of the film shifts from the town to a boat where the three stars track the shark, and vice versa. The creature is no less menacing when finally seen in a fight to the death wherein Shaw fulfills his Captain Ahab destiny.

Bill Butler's Panavision-Technicolor cinematography is excellent; one can almost smell the Martha's Vineyard location. In addition, Rexford Metz did the underwater lensing, while Ron and Valerie Taylor are credited for the live shark footage. The Australian Coral Reef was used for underwater shooting. Robert A. Mattey headed the crew for the diverse and exciting special effects work — including wrecked boats, piers, shark attacks, etc. (A mechanical shark's inanimate temperament was a cause of some filming delays.)

The adroit casting extended through the ranks of supporting players: notably Lorraine Gary (a familiar inhabitant of Universal-TV shows), very good as Scheider's wife; Murray Hamilton, excellent as the temporizing town mayor; scripter Gottlieb as a newspaper editor; Jeffrey C. Kramer, great as Scheider's harried assistant; and author Benchley himself as an eyewitness-type TV newsman.

Verna Fields, since moved on to a senior exec post at Universal, did the topnotch editing, while John Williams' haunting score adds to the mood of impending horror. All other production credits are superior.

The domestic PG rating attests to the fact that implicit dramaturgy is often more effective than explicit carnage.

Murf.

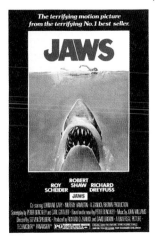

CLOSE ENCOUNTERS OF THE THIRD KIND

Wednesday, November 9, 1977

Special effects overcome flawed story. Big outlook.

Hollywood, Nov. 2. Columbia Pictures release, produced by Julia and Michael Phillips. Written and directed by Steven Spielberg. Features entire cast. Camera (Metrocolor), Vilmos Zsigmond, Douglas Trumbull, William A. Fraker, Douglas Slocombe, John Alonzo, Laszlo Kovacs, Richard Yuricich, Dave Stewart, Robert Hall, Don Jarel, Dennis Muren; second unit camera, Steve Poster; editor, Michael Kahn; music, John Williams; production design, Joe Alves; art direction, Dan Lomino; set decoration, Phil Abramson; sound, Buzz Knudson, Don MacDougall, Robert Glass, Gene Cantamesa, Steve Katz; costumes-wardrobe, Jim Linn; asst. director, Chuck Myers; stunt coordinator, Buddy Joe Hooker. Reviewed at Todd-AO Screening Room, L.A., Nov. 2, '77. (MPAA Rating: PG.) Running time: 135 Mins. (Color).

Roy Neary	Richard Dreyfuss
Claude Lacombe	François Truffaut
Ronnie Neary	Teri Garr
Jillian Guiler	Melinda Dillon
Barry Guiler	Cary Guffey
Interpretor Laughlin	Bob Balaban
Project Leader	J. Patrick McNamara
Wild Bill	Warren Kemmerling
Farmer	Robert Blossom
Jean Claude	Philip Dodds
Neary Children	Shawn Bishop, Adrienne Campbell, Justin Dreyfuss
Robert	Lance Hendricksen
Team Leader	Merrill Connally
Major Benchley	George Dicenzo

"Close Encounters of The Third Kind" is a daring film concept which in its special and technical effects has been superbly realized. Steven Spielberg's film climaxes in final 35 minutes with an almost ethereal confrontation with life forms from another world; the first 100 minutes, however, are somewhat redundant in exposition and irritating in tone. Yet much advance public interest gives the Columbia Pictures-release a strong commercial potential.

The near-$20,000,000 production was shot in Wyoming, Alabama, California and India. Julia Phillips and Michael Phillips produced for Col and partner EMI. Spielberg utilized an enormous crew of creative-technical specialists to achieve some stunning effects which have a cohesion and unity that is, in comparison, lacking somewhat in his screenplay (or at least in the edited form of release prints).

Story involves a series of UFO appearances witnessed by Richard Dreyfuss, Indiana power company technician, and Melinda Dillon and her son Cary Guffey. Concurrent with this plot line are the maneuverings of a seemingly international and secret team of military and scientific personnel in which François Truffaut is a key member.

The early UFO manifestations vividly depict the strong electro-magnetic field exerted on people and objects. Dreyfuss' entire life changes as he gets a fixation for an odd mountain-looking shape that, after overbearing and overdone emphasis, turns out to be Devil's Tower in Wyoming, where the UFOs seem to plan an earthly landing. Separately, Dillon's son is kidnapped by a UFO, giving her a fixation.

Spielberg successfully creates an uneasy tension throughout these first 100 minutes, though the tension eventually is more self-defeating. He has a rather misanthropic viewpoint of contemporary suburbia; add to this a tendency to many closeups (in Panavision, yet) and you have some irritating visual jerkiness;

thrown in what sounds like over-dubbed noise effects, overlapping dialog, a Dreyfuss household consisting of bewildered spouse Teri Garr (her second such casting this season) and three repulsive children, Truffaut talking French through interpreter Bob Balaban, and you have an audio cacophony as well.

Obviously all this was deliberate, to set up the climactic and oddly-pastoral encounter with the humanoids from another world. But the cumulative effect of the earlier audio-visual nightmare – not helped at all by some of the frenzied acting of the principals nor some mob scenes which seem like homage to Billy Wilder's "Ace In The Hole" is to drive at least one viewer to near-distraction. This is unusual in films designed to reach a very broad, blockbuster-type mass audience.

But there's no denying that the climax is an absolute stunner, literate in plotting, dazzling in execution and almost reverent in tone. (It's just as well to forget an implicit vibration here that only in a military – scientific – technocratic dictatorship is there order, discipline and calm.) At the very least the denouement is light years ahead of the climactic nonsense of Stanley Kubrick's "2001—A Space Odyssey." Yet, in terms of real empathy with enduring human nature as it is (warts and all), "Close Encounters" lacks the warmth and humanity of George Lucas' "Star Wars."

Parsing this film is not easy, and various descriptions sound at times negative. But that's the problem: There's no big positive rush here, instead a high-tension, nervous, uneasy, often heartless environment in which Dreyfuss and Dillon, supposedly being the audience's reps in the story, are helpless flotsam. The uncompromising creative point of view, admirable in a professional sense, is pitched to an above-average level of intelligence. Post-release market research, designed to match audience satisfaction to various demographics, could make fascinating reading.

Spielberg takes credit for visual effects concepts, while Douglas Trumbull wears the senior special effects credit. A slew of name cinematographers worked on the film, which began its initial production nearly two years ago. John Williams' score is good; Joe Alves' production design superb.

Breakeven on the film, including marketing costs, is in the area of about $30,000,000 in world rentals, which is a certainty. Between that rental range and the farther limits previously achieved by less than a dozen films, no prudent person can properly venture a guess until a picture begins to actually perform, because the orders of magnitude are too great, not unlike the extra-terrestrial story elements embodied in "Close Encounters" itself. If the film grosses $50,000,000 or $60,000,000 or $100,000,000 or more in world rentals, it will have succeeded at all those levels. The danger in these mega-rental ranges is that nobody yet can tell up front where a film will ultimately burn out.

Murf.

1941

Wednesday, December 19, 1979

Too many bombs, not enuf yocks in Spielberg's World War II spoof. Entertaining film carries some doubts.

Hollywood, Dec. 13. Universal Pictures release of an A-Team production. Produced by Buzz Feitshans. Directed by Steven Spielberg. Exec producer, John Milius. Screenplay, Robert Zemeckis, Bob Gale from a story by Zemeckis Gale, Milius; camera (color), William A. Fraker; editor, Michael Kahn; music, John Williams; production design, Dean Edward Mitzner; sound, Gene S. Cantamessa; special effects, A.D. Flowers; miniature supervisor, Gregory Jein; costumes, Deborah Nadoolman; art direction, William F. O'Brien; matte paintings, Matthew Yuricich; visual effects supervisor, Larry Robinson; production illustrator, George Jensen; set decoration, John Austin; stunt coordinator, Terry Leonard; additional photography, Frank Stanley; choreography, Paul De Rolf; optical consultant, L.B. Abbott; optical effects, Van Der Veer Photo Effects; assistant directors, Jerry Ziesmer, Steve Perry. Reviewed at Directors Guild of America Hollywood, Dec. 11, '79. MPAA Rating: PG. Running time: 118 Mins. (Color).

Sergeant Tree	Dan Aykroyd
Ward Douglas	Ned Beatty
Wild Bill Kelso	John Belushi
Joan Douglas	Lorraine Gary
Claude	Murray Hamilton
Von Kleinschmidt	Christopher Lee
Birkhead	Tim Matheson
Commander Mitamura	Toshiro Mifune
Maddox	Warren Oates
General Stilwell	Robert Stack
Sitarksi	Treat Williams
Donna	Nancy Allen
Herbie	Eddie Deezen
Wally	Bobby DiCicco
Betty	Dianne Kay
Foley	John Candy
Ogden Johnson Jones	Frank McRae
Dennis	Perry Lang
Hollis Wood	Slim Pickens
Maxine	Wendie Jo Sperber
Scioli	Lionel Stander
Meyer Mishkin	Ignatius Wolfington
U.S.O, M.C.	Joseph P. Flaherty

Billed as a comedy spectacle, Steven Spielberg's "1941" is long on spectacle, but short on comedy. The Universal-Columbia Pictures co-production is an exceedingly entertaining, fast-moving revision of 1940s war hysteria in Los Angeles spawned by the bombing of Pearl Harbor, and boasts Hollywood's finest miniature and visual effects work seen to date. Due to the film's frenetic pacing and lack of empathetic characters, however, boxoffice prognosis is not as healthy as that of Spielberg's most recent pix, "Jaws" and "Close Encounters Of The Third Kind."

Another of this year's crop of oft-delayed, bloated-budget spectaculars, "1941" succeeds in many of the goals Spielberg apparently set for himself. It's filled with lavish sight gags, elaborate stunt work, lovely period settings and costumes and a brace of fine thesps. Fact that 82 cast members are specifically credited, along with more than 160 crew and tech personnel in a six-minute end credits crawl, should be ultimate validation that film is a collaborative work.

When all is said and done, however, the vision on the screen is director Spielberg's, giving "1941" both its advantages and its drawbacks. There are few filmmakers who can demonstrate such technical mastery of the medium — Spielberg moves his actors, sets, props and cameras with the efficiency of a creative field marshal.

But "1941" suffers from Spielberg's infatuation with physical comedy, even when the gags involve tanks, planes and submarines, rather than the usual stuff of screen hijinks. Pic is so overloaded with visual humor of a rather monstrous nature that feeling emerges, once you've seen 10 explosions, you've seen them all.

Screenwriters Robert Zemeckis and Bob Gale, who concocted the outlandish storyline in conjunction with exec producer John Milius, are also daring in their attempt to interwine five or six distinct storylines into one coherent tale. Largely this works, thanks to Michael Kahn's fluid editing, John Williams' inspiring and unifying score, and Spielberg's incredible ability to juggle characters and plot turns.

Marquee value of the cast is so top-heavy that some fine performers get lost in the shuffle, through no fault of their own. Dan Aykroyd is very impressive in his feature debut as the serious army sergeant, but his former "Saturday Night Live" cohort John Belushi turns in a snarling, obnoxious performance that simply does not jibe with the rest of the pic.

Real cast standouts are Bobby DiCicco, who spends pic wresting pretty Diane Kay away from horny soldier Treat Williams, Robert Stack as a bemused general, Nancy Allen as the airborne inamorata of Tim Matheson, Wendie Jo Sperber as a frustrated femme and Joseph P. Flaherty as a croony '40s emcee. Christopher Lee and Toshiro Mifune also excel as the bickering Alix powers determined to destroy the only thing of value in Los Angeles, Hollywood, while Ned Beatty, Lorraine Gary, Murray Hamilton and Eddie Deezen are quite good as U.S. citizens who come to their country's aid.

Spielberg also has the sense of humor to spoof his own work in pic's earliest minutes, and flashes of that humor continue intermittently throughout the pic. Main comic appeal, however, resides in whatever audience enjoyment will result from seeing Hollywood Boulevard trashed (in miniature scale), paint factories bulldozed, houses toppled into the sea, and a giant ferris wheel rolling to a watery demise.

Interspersed are some visual and aural delights, particularly a jitterbugging scene set at the Hollywood U.S.O. club, where DiCicco, Kaye and a host of hoofers go through a delightful routine choreographed by Paul De Rolf. There is also a madcap episode involving Warren Oates and his troops expecting an invasion in Barstow, and a touching segment (another Spielberg perennial) in which Stack watches "Dumbo" while the skies of L.A. light up with ack-ack fire.

It hardly matters that the actual "Great Los Angeles Air Raid" took place on Feb. 26, 1942, and not Dec. 13, 1941, as pic's title and setting suggests, nor that some of the racist consequences of that night (along with concurrent Zoot Suit riots) are given short shrift in the film.

What is ultimately lacking from "1941" is that sense of cohesiveness and magic, for lack of a better word, that pulled "Jaws" and "Close Encounters" out of the realm of the ordinary and into the supernatural. No filmmaker should have to carry his previous successes around his neck like a celluloid albatross, of course, but Spielberg's talent is so manifest and dynamic, the pity is that it's not used to better effect here.

In any event, "1941" sets a new screen standard for special effects excellence, particularly with the work of cinematographer William A. Fraker, visual effects supervisor Larry Robinson, designer Dean Edward Mitzner, miniature supervisor Gregory Jein, special effects man A.D. Flowers, optical consultant L.B. Abbott and matte painter Matthew Yuricich.

Also worthy of the highest praise are Deborah Nadoolman's costumes, Gene S.

Cantamessa's superior sound recording and Terry Leonard's disciplined stunt coordinating.

Poll.

RAIDERS OF THE LOST ARK

Wednesday, June 10, 1981

Smashing adventure-fantasy that brings back the good old days. Major b.o. prospects.

A Paramount Pictures release of a Lucasfilm Ltd. Production. Produced by Frank Marshall. Executive producers, George Lucas, Howard Kazanjian. Directed by Steven Spielberg. Features entire cast. Screenplay, Lawrence Kasdan; story, Lucas, Philip Kaufman; associate producer, Robert Watts. Camera (Metrocolor), Douglas Slocombe; music, John Williams; editor, Michael Kahn; production designer, Norman Reynolds; art direction, Leslie Dilley; visual effects supervisor, Richard Edlund. Reviewed at Paramount screening room, N.Y., June 2, 1981. (MPAA Rating: PG) Running time: 115 Mins. (Color)

Indy	Harrison Ford
Marion	Karen Allen
Dietrich	Wolf Kahler
Belloq	Paul Freeman
Toht	Ronald Lacey
Sallah	John Rhys-Davies
Brody	Denholm Elliott
Gobler	Anthony Higgins
Satipo	Alfred Molina
Barranca	Vic Tablian

"Raiders of the Lost Ark" is the stuff that raucous Saturday matinees at the local Bijou once were made of, a cracker jack fantasy-adventure that shapes its pulp sensibilities arid cliff-hanging serial origins into an exhilarating escapist entertainment that will have broad-based summer audiences in the palm of its hand. Even within this summer's hot competitive environment, boxoffice prospects are in the top rank.

Steeped in an exotic atmosphere of lost civilizations, mystical talismans, gritty mercenary adventurers, Nazi arch-villains and ingenious death at every turn, the film is largely patterned on the serials of the 1930s, with a large dollop of Edgar Rice Burroughs.

Story begins in 1936 as Indiana Jones (Harrison Ford), an archaeologist and university professor who's not above a little mercenary activity on the side, plunders a South American jungle tomb. Fending off an awesome array of deadly primitive booby-traps – ranging from light-sensitive poison darts and impaling spikes to legions of tarantulas – he secures a priceless golden Godhead, only to have it snatched away by longtime archaeological rival Paul Freeman, now employed by the Nazis.

Back in the States, Ford is approached by U.S. intelligence agents who tell him the Nazis are rumored to have discovered the location of the Lost Ark of the Covenant (where the broken 10 Commandments were sealed). The ark is assumed to contain an awesome destructive power which Hitler ("he's a nut on the occult," we learn) is intent on using to guarantee his global conquest.

Ford's mission is to beat the Germans to the ark, a trek that takes him first to the mountains of Nepal to retrieve a hieroglyphic medallion that will pinpoint the ark's location, from his onetime flame Karen Allen. Latter, a feisty, hard-drinking spitfire, operates a Nepalese gin-mill; after a massive shootout with medallion-seeking Nazis, the pair wing it to Cairo, where Ford finally makes it to the digging ground.

The action unfolds as a continuing series of exuberantly violent and deadly confrontations – with the Nazis, hired Arab assassins, thousands of venomous snakes that guard the ark, etc., in which Ford miraculously outwits the elements in approved comic strip fashion before fending off the next round of dangers.

As such, the film has some surprisingly explicit violent action and bloodletting for a PG-rated entry and at least one scene (when the Nazis open the ark, liberating Divine fury in the form of spectral beings that melt the defilers' faces and explode their heads into smithereens) that would be attention-getting in an R-rated pic.

Still, for all but the most squeamish that won't detract an iota from the film's overall effect and the virtual start to finish grip of the off-beat tale on its viewers. Lawrence Kasdan's script (exec producer George Lucas and Philip Kaufman penned the original story) spins along the storyline, reveling in all the dialog clichés of the genre without really tipping into self-mockery. Film, cheerfully wearing its improbabilities on its sleeve, is constantly leavened by humor. The kids should love it.

Spielberg has harnessed a perfect balance between escapist fun and hard-edged action, and the film is along the best-crafted ventures of its kind. Suspense components kick in virtually from the first frame onwards, and are maintained throughout the pic.

More important, Spielberg has deftly veiled the entire proceedings in a pervading sense of mystical wonder that makes it all the more easy for viewers to willingly suspend disbelief and settle back for the fun.

Conforming to the traditions of the genre, characterizations are hardly three-dimensional. Still, Ford marks a major turning point in his career as the occasionally frail but ever invincible mercenary-archeologist, projecting a riveting strength of character throughout. Allen's pugnacious personality provides bristling romantic counterpoint and supporting roles (including Ronald Lacey in the most outrageously offensive Nazi stereotype seen on screen since World War II, John Rhys-Davies as Ford's loyal Egyptian helpmate and Denholm Elliott as his university colleague) are all delightfully etched.

Technically, the film is another standard-setter from the Lucas-Spielberg camps (this is their first collaboration), with Douglas Slocombe's lush lensing and John Williams' dramatic score underscoring both the action and the globe-hopping epic scope.

Recruited from the "Star Wars" ranks, production designer Norman Reynolds and art director Leslie Dilley have created a vibrant and period-perfect world of wonders. Michael Kahn's crisp editing keeps the pace and energy unflagging, and Richard Edlund's photographic effects – highlighted by the apocalyptic unveiling of the ark – are intelligently spectacular.

Film's ending leaves the field wide open for a sequel (Lucas already has two more chapters up his sleeve). Hopefully the film's broad commercial promise going in will translate to a large enough bottom-line to keep his Raiders coming for a long time.

Step.

E.T., THE EXTRA-TERRESTRIAL

Wednesday, May 26, 1982

E.T. equals B.O.

Hollywood, May 22. A Universal Pictures production and release. Produced by Steven Spielberg, Kathleen Kennedy. Features entire cast. Directed by Spielberg. Screenplay, Melissa Mathison; camera (Deluxe color), Allen Daviau (prints by Technicolor): editor, Carol Littleton; music, John Williams; production design, James D. Bissell; set decoration, Jackie Carr; assistant director, Katy Emde; E.T. created by Carlo Rambaldi; special visual effects produced at Industrial Light & Magic, supervisor, Dennis Muren; second unit director, Glenn Randall; production manager, Wallace Worsley; production supervisor, Frank Marshall; sound, Gene Cantamessa; supervising sound editor, Charles L. Campbell. Reviewed at Universal Studios, Universal City, May 21, 1982. (MPAA Rating: PG). Running time: 115 Mins. (Color)

Mary	Dee Wallace
Elliott	Henry Thomas
Keys	Peter Coyote
Michael	Robert MacNaughton
Gertie	Drew Barrymore
Greg	K.C. Martel
Steve	Sean Frye
Tyler	Tom Howell
Pretty Girl	Erika Eleniak
Schoolboy	David O'Dell
Science teacher	Richard Swingler
Policeman	Frank Toth
Ultra sound man	Robert Barton
Van man	Michael Darrell

"E.T., The Extra-Terrestrial" may be the best Disney film Disney never made. Captivating, endearingly optimistic and magical at times, Steven Spielberg's fantasy about a stranded alien from outer space protected by three youngsters until it can arrange for passage home is certain to capture the imagination of the world's youth in the manner of most of his earlier pics, as well as those of George Lucas. Result will be a summertime bonanza for distrib Universal. In short, "E.T." equals b.o.

At their best, both Spielberg and Lucas make idealized versions of the kinds of films they loved as kids, in the process furnishing this generation's filmgoers with visual treats of unprecedented skill and sophistication. Despite the continual presence of the little Yoda-like creature, "E.T." is not first and foremost an effects picture, but rather a charming "Twilight Zone" -like fable which reminds by turns of "The Wizard of Oz," "Mary Poppins," a benign switch on "King Kong" and a variation of Spielberg's own "Close Encounters."

Opening sequence actually comes off like a repeat of "Close Encounters" final frames, as a sizeable spaceship takes off just before some earthly authorities are able to close in on it. One of its occupants gets left behind, however, and the viewer is instantly sympathetic with its plight in the threateningly different environment of a modern California subdivision.

E.T. is highly fortunate to be found by young Henry Thomas who, after some understandable initial fright, takes the "goblin" in, first as a sort of pet and then as a friend he must guard against the more preying elements of human society. Over time, Thomas teaches E.T. how to talk and includes his older brother (Robert MacNaughton) and younger sister (Drew Barrymore) in on the secret, even as he manages to hide his discovery from his mother (Dee Wallace).

Ultimately, of course, the official representatives of society locate E.T., which seems to occasion a rapid decline in its health until it appears to die. When it revives, Thomas marshals his friends into a kids' commando squad to spirit E.T. back to the spaceship which is on its way to a rescue rendezvous.

First element which had to work to insure film's success was E.T. itself. As superlatively created by Carlo Rambaldi, the creature manages to project both a wondrous childlike quality and a sense of superior powers. Cutely awkward in its movements, the being has rubbery brown skin, an extendable neck and possesses eyes which dilate on cue. It even gets to play a drunk scene, perhaps a first for screen aliens. Assuredly not lost on those involved with the film are the opportunities for E.T. related toys and dolls, which are enormous.

An amusing sidelight to the tale is that the action takes place in a suburban household almost identical to that in the Spielberg-produced "Poltergeist," which leads to the thought that the two, distinctly different stories could be unfolding in neighboring homes simultaneously. In fact, many of the motifs in the early going are similar to those in "Poltergeist"—the middle-class family, the blonde dog, goldfish, people glaring into bright lights in awe and disbelief.

But "E.T." will surely prove an embraceable film by the general public. Rarely has a picture so completely evinced a kid's p.o.v. and shown the complicity of youngsters against adults. It's been said that the only people who don't like Disneyland are late adolescents who feel too hip to enjoy the pleasures of their earlier years, and the same will probably hold true for "E.T."

As can be expected from Spielberg and the Industrial Light & Magic shop, the technical effects are state-of-the-art superb. Enough cannot be said for John Williams's score, which stands as a model of film composing — although it is almost continually present it's also practically unnoticeable, so well does it both complement and further the events onscreen.

As far as the performances go, the key was finding three kids who could respond with both innocence and gumption to the arrival of E.T. All fulfill the requirements, and Thomas is perfect in the lead, playing the childhood equivalent of Spielberg's everyman heroes of his previous pics.

There are some unsatisfactory elements – slow spots occur during the middle stretch, the mild anti-establishment stance is getting to be a bit of a cliché and one never knows whether E.T.'s mortal illness is physical or psychological in nature, or both. But, as with "Close Encounters," the truly lovely and moving ending more than makes up for everything. Chalk up another smash for Spielberg.

Cart.

TWILIGHT ZONE THE MOVIE

Wednesday, June 15, 1983

Mixed Blessings, but packs a wallop. **Hollywood, June 14. A Warner Bros. release. Produced by Steven Spielberg, John Landis. Executive producer, Frank Marshall. "The Twilight Zone" created by Rod Serling. Music, Jerry Goldsmith; production design, James D. Bissell. Prologue: directed, written by Landis; camera (Technicolor), Steve Larner; editor, Malcolm Campbell; associate producer, George Folsey Jr. Segment 1: directed, written by Landis; camera, Larner; editor, Campbell; associate producer, Folsey; art direction, Richard Sawyer; set decoration, Barbara Paul Krieger; costume design, Deborah Nadoolman; special effects, Paul Stewart: sound, Bill Kaplan; assistant director, Elie Cohn. Segment 2: directed by Spielberg, written by George Clayton Johnson, Richard Matheson, Josh Rogan, from a story by Johnson; camera, Allen Daviau; editor, Michael Kahn; associate producer, Kathleen Kennedy; set design, William J. Teegarden; set decoration, Jackie Carr; sound, Tommy Causey; special effects supervision, Mike Wood; assistant director, Pat Kehoe. Segment 3: directed by Joe Dante, written by Matheson, from a story by Jerome Bixby; camera, John Hora; editor, Tina Hirsch; associate producer, Michael Finnell; set design, Teegarden; set decoration, Carr; sound, Causey; special makeup effects design and creation, Rob Bottin; special effects supervision, Wood; cartoon supervision, Sally Cruikshank; assistant director, Kehoe. Segment 4: directed by George Miller, written by Matheson from his story; camera, Daviau; editor, Howard Smith; associate producer, Jon Davison; art direction, James H. Spencer; set design, Teegarden; set decoration, Carr; sound, Causey; special** makeup effects creation, Craig Reardon, Michael McCracken; special effects supervision, Wood; monster conceptual design, Ed. Verreaux; visual effects, Peter Kuran, Industrial Light & Magic, David Allen; assistant director, Kehoe. Reviewed at the Samuel Goldwyn Theatre, Beverly Hills, May 25, 1983. (MPAA Rating: PG). Running time: 102 Mins. (Color)

Prologue	
Passenger	Dan Aykroyd
Driver	Albert Brooks
Segment 1	
Bill	Vic Morrow
Larry	Doug McGrath
Ray	Charles Hallahan
German Officers	Remus Peets, Kai Wulff
Segment 2	
Mr. Bloom	Scatman Crothers
Mr. Conroy	Bill Quinn
Mr. Weinstein	Martin Garner
Mrs. Weinstein	Selma Diamond
Mrs. Dempsey	Helen Shaw
Mr. Agee	Murray Matheson
Mr. Mute	Peter Brocoo
Miss Cox	Priscilla Pointer
Young Mrs. Weinstein	Tanya Fenmore
Young Mr. Agee	Even Richards
Young Mrs. Dempsey	Laura Mooney
Young Mr. Mute	Christopher Eisenmann
Mr. Grey Panther	Richard Swingler
Mr. Conroy's Son	Alan Haufrect
Daughter-In-Law	Cheryl Secher
Nurse No 2	Elsa Raven
Segment 3	
Helen Foley	Kathleen Quinlan
Anthony	Jeremy Licht
Uncle Walt	Kevin McCarthy
Mother	Patricia Barry
Father	William Schallert
Ethel	Nancy Cartwright

Walter Paisley	Dick Hiller
Sara	Cherie Currie
Tim	Bill Mumy
Charlie	Jeffrey Bannister
Segment 4	
Valentine	John Lithgow
Sr. Stewardess	Abbe Lane
Jr. Stewardess	Donna Dixon
Co-Pilot	John Dennis Johnston
Creature	Larry Cedar
Sky Marshal	Charles Knapp
Little Girl	Christina Nigra
Mother	Lonna Schwab
Old Woman	Margaret Wheeler
Old Man	Eduard Franz
Young Girl	Margaret Fitzgerald
Young Man	Jeffrey Wiesman
Mechanic No.1	Jeffrey Lambert
Mechanic No. 2	Frank Toth

"Twilight Zone — The Movie" plays much like a traditional vaudeville card, what with its tantalizing teaser opening followed by three sketches of increasing quality, all building up to a socko headline act. Feature film spinoff from the late Rod Serling's perennially popular tv series of 20 years ago possesses plenty of built-in want-to-see via title and filming talents involved, but will still have to prove that the segmented, omnibus style encompassing separate stories and casts is not a boxoffice limitation for American audiences, as it normally has been in the past. Biz will assuredly be hefty, although format will probably impose ceiling on this funhouse.

This is also the film, of course, which received, and continues to receive much unwanted publicity in connection with the deaths of actor Vic Morrow and two Vietnamese child thesps. Some trade talk in the intervening months has centered on whether or not the fatal helicopter accident would cast a pall over the entire project and, indeed, there was considerable internal discussion over the possibility of jettisoning the entire John Landis episode because of it. As has been reported, sequence involving the chopper and kids is nowhere to be seen, and trade awareness of the tragedy and its aftermath may foster a distorted impression of its looming importance to the public at large.

Pic consists of prolog by Landis as well as vignettes, none running any longer than original tv episodes by Landis, Steven Spielberg, Joe Dante and George Miller, all of whom have previously evinced an affinity for the fantasy, sci-fi and/or horror genres. Ironically, the lesser known of the quartet, Dante and Miller, manage to shine the brightest in this context, a fact which will considerably raise their stock in the industry.

Landis gets things off to a wonderful start with a comic prolog starring Dan Aykroyd and Albert Brooks. Driving down a deserted highway, they engagingly shoot the breeze, sing some tunes and discuss, with no self-consciousness whatever favorite "Twilight Zone" episodes before Aykroyd shows Brooks something "really scary." Placing entire "Twilight Zone" phenomenon in cultural context, sequence ideally sets up the feature as a whole.

Landis' principal episode, however, is a downbeat, one-dimensional fable about racial and religious intolerance. An embittered, middleaged man who has just been passed over for a job promotion, Morrow sports a torrent of racial epithets aimed at Jews, Blacks and Orientals while drinking with buddies at a bar. Upon exiting, he finds himself in Nazi-occupied Paris as a suspected Jew on the run from the Gestapo. After a prolonged chase and brush with death, he is then transported to the American South, where Ku Klux Klan is about to lynch him. In short order, he is plopped down in Vietnam, where both the Yanks and the Viet Cong threatened his

existence. Back in Paris, he is rounded up with a crowd of Jews for shipment to a concentration camp.

Intent is noble and dramatic situations faced by Morrow are intense, but having made its only point early on, sequence misses the sort of catharsis which was reportedly part of the story to begin with, wherein the bigoted man would experience a change of heart. Desperately sweaty throughout, Morrow strongly conveys the insecurity lying shallow beneath the character's aggressive hatefulness, but dramatic payoff is thin.

This is the only sequence in the film not derived from an actual tv episode, although it does bear a thematic resemblance to a 1961 installment titled "A Quality Of Mercy," in which Dean Stockwell portrayed a marauding American lieutenant in the Philippines during World War II who is changed into a besieged Japanese soldier on Corregidor.

Based on the episode originally called "Kick The Can" (none of the segments are given titles in the feature), Spielberg's entry is sweetly sentimental and quite the most down-to-earth of all the stories.

In a retirement home filled with oldsters living in the past, spry Scatman Crothers encourages various residents to think young and, in organizing a game of kick the can, actually transforms them into their childhood selves again.

Filmette is filled with delightful characterizations by both the old and young performers, and is entirely recognizable as a Spielberg work via the sense of awe and wonder expressed by the characters as they recapture a childhood p.o.v. of the world. But despite fact that no theme could be closer to the director's heart, sequence has the air of pencil sketch rather than a fully-painted picture, and impact is no more than lightly charming. Jerry Goldsmith, who provides strong and varied music for the entire film, has come up with scoring for Spielberg which sounds for all the world like that of John Williams, and emotionally it peaks far too soon in the tale.

Most bizarre contribution comes from Joe Dante, who wrings considerable changes on a story first called "It's A Good Life." Outsider Kathleen Quinlan enters the Twilight Zone courtesy of little Jeremy Licht, who lords it over a Looney-Tune household by virtue of his power to will anything into existence except happiness.

Afraid of what the young progeny might unleash upon them, Licht's family grovels before him in exaggerrated 1950s tv style, and house itself is a masterpiece of expressionistic art direction in the manners of "The Cabinet Of Dr. Caligari."

Classic cartoons are forever playing on tv in the background, and payoff comes when he brings some of the more monstrous cartoon characters to life in the living room. It's a unique and startling sequence, one which also contains the most sustained explosion of special effects in the entire film.

For the record, Billy Mumy, who played the boy on tv, can be seen in a preliminary roadside diner scene, as can Dick Miller in a reprise of his Walter Paisley characterization.

But, wisely, the best has been saved for last. George Miller's re-working of "Nightmare at 20,000 Feet," about a man who sees a gremlin tearing up an engine wing of an airplane, is electrifying from beginning to end. This Australian and former medic proved with "Mad Max" and "The Road Warrior" that he is the most talented action director to have come down the pike in years, and now he has created another amazing work in his first shot in Hollywood.

Dropping the character of the man's wife, Miller zeroes right in on the fully justifiable paranoia of John Lithgow, who grows increasingly crazed as he, and only he among the passengers and crew, catches glimpses of the monster wreaking havoc on the aircraft as it flies through a storm.

Rarely has the sense of movement in flight been so strongly evoked, and lensing and editing superbly contribute to rapidly building tension throughout the sequence which passes like wind. Furthermore, Lithgow brilliantly delineates the deteriorating mental state of a man into whom all can project their own fear of flying.

Only flaw lies in the realm of nit-picking — exterior of the plane is an old Boeing 707, while interior is of the widebody variety.

Burgess Meredith, who acted in more than one "Twilight Zone" episode, has provided some introductory remarks, while the familiar recording of Serling is laid in at conclusion.

Overall, pic is a mixed bag of mostly moderate pleasures which has been expertly, and not too lavishly, produced.

For the record, original "Kick The Can" episode was written by George Clayton Thomas and directed by Lamont Johnson. "It's A Good Life" was penned by Serling from a Jerome Bixby short story, and was directed by James Shelton. "Nightmare at 20,000 feet," adapted from his own story by Richard Matheson, who has contributed heavily to the feature, was directed by Richard Donner.

Cart.

INDIANA JONES AND THE TEMPLE OF DOOM

Wednesday, May 16, 1984

Noisy, overkill prequel headed for smash b.o.

Hollywood, May 7. A Paramount Pictures release of a Lucas-film Ltd. production. Executive producers, George Lucas, Frank Marshall. Produced by Robert Watts. Directed by Steven Spielberg. Stars Harrison Ford. Screenplay, Willard Huyck, Gloria Katz, from a story by Lucas. Camera (Rank color; prints by Deluxe), Douglas Slocombe; editor, Michael Kahn; music, John Williams; sound design (Dolby), Ben Burtt; production design, Elliot Scott; chief art director, Alan Cassie; set decoration, Peter Howitt; special visual effects supervisor, Dennis Muren at Industrial Light & Magic; costume design, Anthony Powell; mechanical effects supervisor, George Gibbs; second unit director, Michael Moore; choreography, Danny Daniels; associate producer, Kathleen Kennedy. Reviewed at MGM Studios, Culver City, Calif., May 7, 1984. (MPAA Rating: PG). Running time: 118 Mins. (Color)

Indiana Jones	Harrison Ford
Willie Scott	Kate Capshaw
Short Round	Ke Huy Quan
Mola Ram	Amrish Puri
Chattar Lal	Roshan Seth
Capt. Blumburtt	Philip Stone

Also with: Roy Chiao, David Yip, Ric Young, Chua Kah Joo, Rex Ngui, Philip Tann, Dan Aykroyd, Pat Roach.

Special Visual Effects Unit Credits

Industrial Light & Magic; visual effects supervisor, Dennis Muren; chief cameraman, Mike McAlister; optical photography supervisor, Bruce Nicholson; ILM general manager, Tom Smith; production supervisor, Warren Franklin; matte painting supervisor, Michael Pangrazio; modelship supervisor, Lorne Peterson; stop-motion animation, Tom St. Amand; supervising stage technician, Patrick Fitzsimmons; animation supervisor, Charles Mullen; supervising editor, Howard Stein; production coordinator, Arthur Repola; creative consultant, Phil Tippett. Additional optical effects, Modern Film Effects.

Additional Technical Credits

U.K.crew: assistant director, David Tomblin; production supervisor, John Davis; production manager, Patricia Carr. U.S. crew: production manager, Robert Latham Brown; assistant director, Louis Race. first unit: stunt arrangers, Vic Armstrong (studio), Glenn Randall (location); additional photography, Paul Beeson; sound mixer, Simon Kaye; chief modeller, Derek Howart; chief special effects technician, Richard Conway; floor effects supervisor, David Watkins; research, Deborah Fine; post-production services, Sprocket Systems.

London second unit: second unit director, Frank Marshall; assistant directors, David Bracknell, Michael Hook; cameraman, Wally Byatt; floor effects supervisor, David Harris.

California Unit: second unit director, Glenn Randall; director of photography, Allen Daviau; art direction, Joe Johnston; stunt coordinator, Dean Raphael Ferrandini; special effects supervisor, Kevin Pike; sound mixer, David McMillan; production coordinator, Lata Ryan.

Asian unit: assistant director, Carlos Gil. Macau: production supervisor, Vincent Winter; production manager, Pay Ling Wang; assistant director, Patty Chan. Sri Lanka: production supervisor, Chandran Rutnam; production manager, Willie de Silva; assistant director, Ranjit H. Peiris; steadicam photography, Garrett Brown; art direction, Errol Kelly; sound mixer, Colin Charles.

Aerial unit: second unit director, Kevin Donnelly; director of photography, Jack Cooperman.

Just as "Return Of The Jedi" seemed disappointing after the first two "Star Wars" entries, so does "Indiana Jones And The Temple Of Doom" come as a letdown after "Raiders Of The Lost Ark." This is ironic, because director Steven Spielberg has packed even more thrills and chills into this followup than he did into the earlier pic, but to exhausting and numbing effect.

End result is like the proverbial Chinese meal, where heaps of food can still leave one hungry shortly thereafter. Will any of this make any difference at the boxoffice? Not a chance, as a sequel to "Raiders," which racked up $112,000,000 in domestic film rentals, has more built-in want-see than any imaginable film aside from "E.T. II."

Spielberg, scenarists Willard Huyck and Gloria Katz, and George Lucas, who penned the story as well as exec producing with Frank Marshall, have not tampered with the formula which made "Raiders" so popular. To the contrary, they have noticeably stepped up the pace, amount of incidents, noise level, budget, close calls, violence and everything else, to the point where more is decidedly less.

Prequel finds dapper Harrison Ford as Indiana Jones in a Shanghai night-club in 1935, and title sequence, which features Kate Capshaw chirping Cole Porter's "Anything Goes," looks like something out of Spielberg's "1941".

Ford escapes from an enormous melee with the chanteuse in tow and, joined by Oriental moppet Ke Huy Quan, they head by plane to the mountains of Asia, where they are forced to jump out in an inflatable raft, skid down huge slopes, vault over a cliff and navigate some rapids before coming to rest in an impoverished Indian village.

Community's leader implores the ace archaeologist to retrieve a sacred, magical stone which has been stolen by malevolent neighbors, so the trio makes its way by elephant to the domain of a prepubescent Maharajah, who lords it over an empire reeking of evil.

Remainder of the yarn is set in this labyrinth of horrors, where untold dangers await the heroes. Much of the action unfolds in a stupendous cavern, where dozens of natives chant wildly as a sacrificial victim has his heart removed before being lowered into a pit of fire.

Ford is temporarily converted to the nefarious cause, Ke Huy Quan is sent to join child slaves in an underground quarry, and Capshaw is lowered time and again into the pit until the day is saved.

What with John Williams' incessant score and the library full of sound effects, there isn't a quiet moment in the entire picture, and the filmmakers have piled one giant setpiece on top of another to the point where one never knows where it will end.

Film's one genuinely amazing action sequence, not unlike the airborne sleigh chase in "Jedi" (the best scene in that film), has the three leads in a chase on board an underground railway car on tracks resembling those of a roller-coaster.

Sequence represents a stunning display of design, lensing and editing, and will have viewers gaping. A "Raidersland" amusement park could be opened profitably on the basis of this ride alone.

Overall, however, pic comes on like a sledgehammer, and there's even a taste of vulgarity and senseless excess not apparent in "Raiders."

Kids 10-12 upwards will eat it all up, of course, but many of the images, particularly those involving a gruesome feast of live snakes, fried beetles, eyeball soup and monkey brains, and those in the sacrificial ceremony, might prove extraordinarily frightening to younger children who, indeed, are being catered to in this film by the presence of the adorable 12-year-old Ke Huy Quan.

Compared to the open-air breeziness of "Raiders", "Indiana Jones," after the first reel or so, possesses a heavily studio-bound look, with garish reds often illuminating the dark backgrounds.

As could be expected, however, huge production crew at Thorn EMI-Elstree Studios, as well as those on locations in Sri Lanka, Macao and California and in visual effects phase at Industrial Light & Magic, have done a tremendous job in rendering this land of high adventure and fantasy.

Ford seems effortlessly to have picked up where he left off when Indiana Jones was last heard from, (though tale is set in an earlier period), although Capshaw, who looks fetching in native attire, has unfortunately been asked to react hysterically to everything that happens to her, resulting in a manic, frenzied performance which never locates a center of gravity. Villains are all larger-than-life nasties.

Critical opinion is undoubtedly irrelevant for such a surefire commercial attraction as "Indiana Jones," except that Spielberg is such a talented director it's a shame to see him lose all sense of subtlety and nuance.

In one quick step, the "Raiders" films have gone the way the James Bond opuses went at certain points, away from nifty stories in favor of one big effect after another. But that won't prevent Spielberg and Lucas from notching another mark high on the list of all-time b.o. winners.

Cart.

THE COLOR PURPLE

Wednesday, December 18, 1985

Overproduced, overly manipulative Steven Spielberg Drama is saved by outstanding performances.

Hollywood, Dec. 11. A Warner Bros. release of an Amblin Entertainment presentation, in association with Quincy Jones. A Guber-Peters Co. production. Produced by Steven Spielberg, Kathleen Kennedy, Frank Marshall, Quincy Jones. Executive producers, Jon Peters, Peter Guber. Directed by Spielberg. Features entire cast. Screenplay by Menno Meyjes, based on the novel by Alice Walker; camera (DeLuxe color), Allen Daviau; editor, Michael Kahn; music, Quincy Jones; production design, J. Michael Riva; set decorator, Linda DeScenna; art director, Robert W. Welch; sound, Willie Burton; costume design, Aggie Guerard Rodgers; assistant director, Pat Kehoe, Richard Alexander Wells; second unit director, Frank Marshall; stunt coordinator, Greg W. Elam; associate producer, Carol Isenberg; casting, Reuben Cannon and Associates. Reviewed at Samuel Goldwyn Theatre, Beverly Hills, Calif., Dec. 10, 1985. (MPAA Rating: PG-13.) Running time: 152 Mins. (Color)

Albert	Danny Glover
Celie	Whoopi Goldberg
Shug Avery	Margaret Avery
Sofia	Oprah Winfrey
Harpo	Willard Pugh
Nettie	Akosua Busia
Young Celie	Desreta Jackson
Old Mr	Adolph Caesar
Squeak	Rae Dawn Chong
Miss Millie	Dana Ivey

There are some great scenes and great performances in "The Color Purple," but it is not a great film. Steven Spielberg's turn at "serious" filmmaking is marred in more than one place by overblown production that threatens to drown in its own emotions. But the characters created in Alice Walker's novel are so vivid that even this doesn't kill them off and there is still much to applaud (and cry about) here. Boxoffice outlook is promising without approaching other Spielberg superhits.

Comparisons to Walker's novel are inevitable and it seems safe to say that those who haven't read the book will be more favorably disposed to the film. It is not that the film need slavishly recreate the book – no film does. It is more a question of whether the film preserves and translates what made the book special and the answer here is yes, and no.

Much of what is successful in the film is from the book. Walker has created truly memorable characters and some very touching scenes. Some of them have made it onto film while other are missing. Overall, the film lacks the depth, variety and richness of the book.

Walker's tale is the story of a black family's growth and flowering over a 40-year period in the south starting around 1909. At the center of everything is Celie, who as a young girl gives birth to two children and is then married into a life of virtual servitude to a man she can refer to only as "Mr." (Danny Glover).

Above all "The Color Purple" is a love story between Celie and her sister, Nettie, from whom she is separated at childhood, and, later in life, the blues singer Shug Avery. It is the love which holds together the extended family and the loosely structured narrative. Unfortunately the script by Menno Meyjes doesn't bind the lives together well enough and the film often feels cluttered with too much going on in too small a space.

Relationship between Celie and Shug as written by Walker is a complex and deeply felt friendship fueled, in part, by a strong sexual attraction. While

Spielberg touches on this it remains pretty much in the background.

Shug is a wonderful Bessie Smith-type character who Celie is attracted to because of her pure joy for living. For Celie, her love for Shug is her lifeblood but the film never dares to get under her skin to feel its heat. As a result one of the central relationships of the story is weakened.

As for the other crucial relationship between the sisters, Nettie is basically not heard from for the first half of the film because Mr. is not giving her letters to Celie. The film finally comes alive when Celie stands up for herself at a family dinner and claims the letters and her freedom.

Things also pick up with the reentry of Nettie (Akosua Busia) into the picture. She has spent years as a missionary in Africa where, through a strange twist of fate, she has been raising Celie's children. Cross-cutting between Africa and Georgia draws some interesting visual and cultural parallels between the two lives.

Other isolated scenes are striking but they don't pack much emotional wallop until the last half hour when the scales of justice are balanced. Subplot involving Mr.'s son Harpo (Willard Pugh) and his bossy wife Sofia (Oprah Winfrey) are good examples of the struggle for family power playing itself out a generation later.

There are few surprises in the story and Spielberg leans heavily on all the key emotional scenes so that the audience knows what to feel and what's coming. Music by coproducer Quincy Jones reenforces the cues set up by Spielberg, although the score is much more subtle and affecting in the African segments.

Spielberg has smoothed out most of the rough edges giving the film a rather limited emotional range. There are numerous shots of the Georgia landscape dusted with snow and portentous shots of the mailbox waiting for news from Nettie. The emotional notes are familiar, sometimes they ring true, more often they seem manipulated and overstated.

Texture of Southern black life is well drawn, if a bit too perfect and homogenized. J. Michael Riva's period production design looks authentic and Aggie Guerard Rodgers' costumes are lovely but perhaps too numerous. These people seem to be doing a lot better than simply eking out a living.

Saving grace of the film are the performances. As the adult Celie debuting Whoopi Goldberg uses her expressive face and joyous smile to register the character's growth. Equally good is Glover who is a powerful screen presence. He is however, too likeable to suggest the evilness of his character, but here, even more than in Walker's novel, no one is truly evil.

Other standouts include Oprah Winfrey's burly Sofia and Margaret Avery's spicy Shug Avery. Rae Dawn Chong as Harpo's girlfriend Squeak is one of the casualties of the film with little remaining of her part. She is one of several fringe characters whom seem to come and go without much holding them to the story.

Tech credits are outstanding. The film looks great. Allen Daviau's photography is bright and colorful aided by Michael Kahn's snappy editing which is exceptional at melding images together.

Ultimately, "The Color Purple" is not that different from other Spielberg pictures despite the setting. It comes out as a fairy tale of black life in the South where family and friends can live in peace and harmony happily ever after. It is an appealing fantasy, if it were only true.

Jagr.

EMPIRE OF THE SUN

Wednesday, December 2, 1987

Spielberg spectacular lacks precision. B.O. outlook okay.

A Warner Bros. release of a Robert Shapiro production from Amblin Entertainment. Produced by Steven Spielberg, Kathleen Kennedy, Frank Marshall. Executive producer, Shapiro. Directed by Spielberg. Screenplay, Tom Stoppard, based on the novel by J.G. Ballard; camera (Technicolor), Allen Daviau; editor, Michael Kahn; music, John Williams; production design, Norman Reynolds; supervising art director, Charles Bishop, Maurice Fowler (China); Norman Dorme (Spain); art direction, Frederick Hole; set decoration, Harry Cordwell, Michael D. Ford; costume design, Bob Ringwood; sound (Dolby), Colin Charles, Tony Dawe; special effects supervisor, Kit West; additional optical effects, Industrial Light & Magic, Dennis Muren, Michael Pangrazio, John Ellis; associate producer, Chris Kenny; assistant director, David Tomblin; casting, Maggie Cartier, Mike Fenton-Jane Feinberg, Judy Taylor (U.S.), Yuriko Matsubara (Japan); second unit director, Frank Marshall; second unit camera, Jimmy Devis. Reviewed at The Burbank Studios, Burbank, Calif., Nov. 24, 1987. (MPAA Rating: PG.) Running time: 152 Mins. (Color)

Jim	Christian Bale
Basie	John Malkovich
Mrs. Victor	Miranda Richardson
Dr. Rawlins	Nigel Havers
Frank Demerest	Joe Pantoliano
Maxton	Leslie Phillips
Sgt. Nagata	Masato Ibu
Jim's Mother	Emily Richard
Jim's Father	Rupert Frazer
Mr. Victor	Peter Gale

Kamikaze Boy Pilot	Takatoro Kataoka
Dainty	Ben Stiller
Tiptree	David Neidorf
Cohen	Ralph Seymour
Mr. Lockwood	Robert Stephens

Hollywood — Steven Spielberg delves deeply into the well of seriousness in "Empire Of The Sun" and comes up with about half-a-bucket. Story of an 11-year-old boy stranded in Japanese-occupied China during World War II seems tailor-made for Spielberg's fantastical inclinations as well as his increasing artistic ambition, and sweeping picture is studded by spectacular set pieces, many staged on location in and around Shanghai. Young Christian Bale successfully carries this massive production on his small shoulders, and focus on this bright, energetic fellow, along with the Spielberg name, should guarantee good initial business. But length, sketchy characterizations, pronounced Britishness and lack of a strong narrative might well keep ultimate b.o. at a lower level than is customary for the director.

With this and "The Last Emperor" entering release, much will be made of China's current fashionability on world screens. Nevertheless, "Empire Of The Sun" actually represents an ideal companion piece to "Hope And Glory," in that both are about how young boys left to their own devices can have a bloody marvelous, adventurous time during a catastrophic war.

Although the most striking single feature of "Empire" is its central situation, Spielberg has not striven to make a realistic or historically complex film. J.G. Ballard's autobiographical 1984 novel marked the first non-science-fiction book by the author, and both it and the film clearly are the work of sci-fi artists channelling their imaginations into a more traditional framework.

Leading the first troupe of Hollywood studio filmmakers ever into Shanghai, a city virtually unchanged since the events depicted, Spielberg turns the grey metropolis into a sensational film set as he delineates the edginess and growing chaos leading up to Japan's entry into the city just after Pearl Harbor.

Jim is in every way a proper upper-class English lad but for the fact he has never seen England. Like many a Spielberg leading boy, he dreams of the skies and the vehicles that can take him there, in this case wartime airplanes.

Separated from his parents during the spectacularly staged evacuation of Shanghai, Jim makes do for a while on his own before hooking up with a pair of American scavengers, with whom in due course he is rounded up and sent to a prison camp for the duration of the war.

It is there that Jim flourishes, expending his boundless energy on creative projects and pastimes that finally land him a privileged place among the entrepreneurially minded Americans. He's a go-getter and a survivor, and the war, which represents his "University of Life," leads him to grow in many ways that his previous cloistered existence would never have permitted.

Except for its basic intelligence, there is no recognizing the stamp of brilliant playwright Tom Stoppard in the screenplay. Much more visible is the virtual inventory of Spielberg touches – the obsession with flight, the bicycle riding, the attempts at revival of the dead, the looks of awe, the heavily backlit E.T. fingers and the amassed loot of the world out of "Raiders Of The Lost Ark" (and "Citizen Kane").

Jim's alert inventiveness in the face of adversity is the hallmark of the story, although the point of it all by the end seems fuzzy. Picture is composed mainly of vivid vignettes stemming from the confined situation, but there is little feeling of years passing or people changing.

When Jim's anticipated reunion with his parents approaches, one doesn't know whether to feel emotional relief or sadness that his life probably will once again become conventional.

John Malkovich's Basie, an opportunistic King Rat type, keeps threatening to become a fully developed character but never does, although the man remains interesting and the actor's sly, insinuating line regarding frequently conjure up thoughts of Jack Nicholson.

Otherwise, the characters are complete blanks, which severely limits the emotional reverberation of the piece. No special use is made of the talents of Miranda Richardson, Nigel Havers, Joe Pantoliano and the others, so it is up to young English thesp Christian Bale to engage the viewer's interest, which he does superbly with a living performance graced by an appealing gravity.

Noteworthy, too, is the attitude toward the Japanese. Although they are the invaders and masters of the prison camp, Jim admires them for their bravery and flying skills, saluting them on occasion and forming a special bond with a young pilot. On balance, the Japanese comes off more favorably than the grubby Yanks, and surely no American film depicting Japanese behavior during World War II, especially towards prisoners, has adopted so benign an attitude toward our then-enemies.

Novel and script provides numerous opportunities for wild surrealism, notably in the area of contrast between Western fashion and Eastern convention, and Spielberg follows up on them, even if his natural instincts don't lie in this direction. One suspects a European director would have emphasized the harshness and absurdism of the situation, but Spielberg still has pulled off some riveting scenes, such as Jim secretly watching a couple beginning to make love as Shanghai is bombed in the distance, and an atom bomb blast being observed from 500 miles away.

The gritty backstreets of Shanghai and heavy facades along the Bund on the waterfront are used to maximum effect by the director, who actually got to shoot in China for only three weeks. Spectacular prison camp set was built in Spain, while other scenes were shot in the U.K.

All technical contributions are, almost by definition, monumentally good. Allen Daviau's lensing, Norman Reynold's production design, Michael Kahn's editing and John Williams' lush score are all top drawer, and a few special effects shots lend the picture added scope. Overall, this is a terrifically ambitious work, partially, but still imposingly, achieved.

Cart.

INDIANA JONES AND THE LAST CRUSADE

May 24–30, 1989

Hollywood. A Paramount Pictures release of a Lucasfilm Ltd. production. Executive producers, George Lucas, Frank Marshall. Produced by Robert Watts. Production executive (U.S.), Kathleen Kennedy. directed by Steven Spielberg. Screenplay, Jeffrey Boam, from a story by Lucas, Menno Meyjes, based on characters created by Lucas and Philip Kaufman; camera (Rank color), Douglas Slocombe; additional photography, Paul Beeson, Robert Stevens; editor, Michael Kahn; music, John Williams; sound (Dolby), Ben Burtt; production design, Elliot Scott; art direction, Stephen Scott, Richard Berger (U.S.), Benjamin Fernandez (Spain), Guido Salsilli (Italy); set design, Alan Kaye (U.S.); set decorators, Peter Howitt, Ed McDonald (U.S.), Julian Mateos (Spain); visual effects supervisor, Michael J. McAlister, Industrial Light & Magic; mechanical effects supervisor, George Gibbs; costume design, Anthony Powell, Joanna Johnston; makeup supervisor, Peter Robb-King; stunt coordinator, Vic Armstrong; associate producer, Arthur Repola; assistant directors, David Tomblin (U.K.), Dennis Maguire (U.S.), Carlos Gil, Jose Luis Escolar (Spain), Gianni Cozzo (Italy); second-unit directors, Michael Moore, Frank Marshall; second-unit camera, Rex Metz (U.S.); second-unit assistant director, Gareth Tandy (U.K.); production supervisor, Patricia Carr (U.K.); unit production managers, Roy Button (U.K.), Joan Bradshaw, Ian Bryce (U.S.), Denise O'Dell (Spain); location managers, Bruce Rush (U.S.), Christopher Hamilton (Italy); casting, Maggie Cartier, Mike Fenton, Judy Taylor, Valerie Massalas. Reviewed at Mann National theater, L.A., May 16, 1989. MPAA Rating: PG-13. Running time: 127 Mins.

Indiana Jones	Harrison Ford
Professor Henry Jones	Sean Connery
Marcus Brody	Denholm Elliott
Elsa	Alison Doody
Sallah	John Rhys-Davies
Walter Donovan	Julie Glover
Young Indy	River Phoenix
Vogel	Michael Byrne
Kazim	Kevork Malikyan
Grail Knight	Robert Eddison
Fedora	Richard Young
Sultan	Alexei Sayle
Young Henry	Alex Hyde-White
Panama Hat	Paul Maxwell

To Say that Paramount's "Indiana Jones And The Last Crusade" may be the best film ever made for 12-year-olds is not a backhanded compliment. What was conceived as a child's dream of a Saturday matinee serial has evolved into a moving excursion into religious myth.

More cerebral than the first two Indiana Jones films, and less schmaltzy than the second, this literate adventure should make big bucks by entertaining and enlightening kids and adults.

The Harrison Ford-Sean Connery father-and-son team gives "Last Crusade" unexpected emotional depth, reminding us that real film magic is not in special effects.

For Lucas and Spielberg, who are now entering middle age, the fact that this is more a character film than f/x extravaganza could signal a welcome new level of ambition.

Jeffrey Boam's witty and laconic screenplay, based on a story by Lucas and Menno Meyjes, takes Ford and Connery on a quest for a prize bigger than the Lost Ark of the covenant — The Holy Grail.

Connery is a medieval lit prof with strong religious convictions who has spent his life assembling clues to the grail's whereabouts. Father and more intrepid archaeologist son piece them together in an around-the-world adventure, leading to a touching and mystical finale that echoes "Star Wars" and "Lost Horizon." The love between father and son transcends even the quest for the Grail, which is guarded by a special 700-year-old knight beautifully played by Robert Eddison.

This film minimizes the formulaic love interest, giving newcomer Alison Doody an effectively sinuous but decidedly secondary role. The principal love story is between father and son, making Ford's casually sadistic personality more sympathetic than in the previous pics.

The relationship between the men is full of tension, manifesting itself in Connery's amusing sexual one-upmanship and his string of patronizing putdowns.

There's also a warmth and growing respect between them that makes this one of the most pleasing screen pairings since Newman met Redford.

Connery confidently plays his aging character as slightly daft and fuzzy-minded, without blunting his forcefulness and without sacrificing his sexual charisma.

The cartoonlike Nazi villains of "Raiders" have been replaced by more genuinely frightening Nazis led by Julian Glover and Michael Byrne. Most of the film takes place in 1938, and Spielberg stages a chilling scene at a Nazi book-burning rally in Berlin, where Ford has a brief encounter with Adolf Hitler.

But exec producers Lucas and Frank Marshall, producer Robert Watts and Spielberg do not neglect the action set-pieces that give these films their commercial cachet.

There's the opening chase on top of a train in the Utah desert, involving a youthful Indy (River Phoenix) in 1912; a ferocious tank battle in the desert; a ghastly scene with hundreds of rats in a Venice catacomb; some aerial hijinks with a zeppelin and small planes, and many more outlandish scenes.

Perhaps the film's most impressive technical aspect is the soundtrack, designed by Ben Burtt. While the noise level sometimes becomes painful, the artistry is stunning.

Douglas Slocombe's lensing has a subtly burnished look, and Elliot Scott's production design is always spectacular.

The Industrial Light & Magic visual effects — supervised by Michael J. McAlister with Patricia Blau producing for the aerial unit — are artful and seamless.

John Williams' score again is a major factor in the appeal and pacing, and editor Michael Kahn makes the film move like a bullet. Other tech contributions are impeccable.

This is a film of which Lucas and Spielberg and their collaborators long will be proud.

Mac.

ALWAYS

December 20, 1989

Hollywood. A Universal Pictures release of a Universal/United Artists presentation from Amblin Entertainment. Produced by Steven Spielberg, Frank Marshall, Kathleen Kennedy. Coproducer, Richard Vane. Directed by Spielberg. Screenplay, Jerry Belson, based on film "A Guy Named Joe," with screenplay by Dalton Trumbo, adaptation by Frederick Hazlitt Brennan, story by Chandler Sprague, David Boehm; camera (Deluxe color), Mikael Salomon; editor, Michael Kahn; music, John Williams; sound (Dolby), Willie Burton; production design, James Bissell; art direction, Chris Burian-Mohr, Richard Reynolds (Montana), Richard Fernandez (Washington); set design, Carl Stensel; set decoration, Jackie Carr; costume design, Ellen Mirojnick; sound design, Ben Burtt; visual effects, Industrial Light & Magic; visual effects supervisor, Bruce Nicholson; visual effects producer, Jim Morris; visual effects camera, Hiro Narita; special effects supervisor, Mike Wood; aerial sequence design, Joe Johnston; forest fire plates director, Bissell; additional aerial sequence director, James Gavin; aerial unit camera, Frank Holgate, Alexander Witt; underwater camera, Peter Romano; assistant director, Pat Kehoe; 2d unit director, Marshall; 2d unit additional camera, John Toll, Gary Graver; casting, Lora Kennedy. Reviewed at Universal Studios, Hollywood, Dec. 8, 1989. MPAA Rating: PG. Running time: 121 Mins.

Pete Sandich	Richard Dreyfuss
Dorinda Durston	Holly Hunter
Ted Baker	Brad Johnson
Al Yackey	John Goodman
Hap	Audrey Hepburn
Dave	Roberts Blossom
Powerhouse	Keith David
Nails	Ed Van Nuys
Rachel	Mary Helgenberger
Bus driver	Doug McGrath
The Singer	J.D. Souther

Not every Steven Spielberg film can or should be a grandiose cinematic event. The kind of film he would have made if he had been a studio contract director during Hollywood's golden era, "Always" is a relatively small-scale engagingly casual, somewhat silly, but always entertaining fantasy.

Richard Dreyfuss charmingly inherits the lead role of a pilot returned from the dead in this re-make of the 1943 Spencer Tracy pic "A Guy Named Joe" set among firefighters in national parks. The Universal release may not reach the b.o. stratosphere, but should be a high flier, nevertheless.

The fondly remembered original film, scripted by Dalton Trumbo and directed by Victor Fleming, used the omnipresence of death in World War II to give emotional weight to Tracy's self-sacrificing beyond-the-grave encouragement of the romance between bereaved flame Irene Dunne and tyro flier Van Johnson, who also benefits from his tutelage in the air.

Spielberg's transposition of the story to the spectacularly burning Montana forests – incorporating footage shot during the devastating 1988 fires at Yellowstone National Park – is a valid equivalent, for the most part, especially since his action sequences using old World War II-era planes are far more thrilling than those of "A Guy Named Joe," whose strengths are more in its character relationships.

The supernatural elements of "Always" may cause some tittering. In place of the fliers' heaven in "Joe," with starchy commanding officer Lionel Barrymore giving Tracy a moving pep talk on his role in the war effort, Spielberg has nothing more to offer than a fey sylvan afterlife supervised by bromide-spouting Audrey Hepburn. She's alluring as always, but corny as a live-action fairy godmother.

Holly Hunter's dispatcher and semi-skilled aspiring pilot, lacking the womanly grace Dunne brought to the part, comes off as gawky and ditzy in the early parts of "Always." Bereavement seems to visibly mature the actress, whose emotional struggle between the memory of Dreyfuss and new love Brad Johnson becomes spirited and gripping.

Original Film
A Guy Named Joe

Metro release of Everett Riskin production. Stars Spencer Tracy and Irene Dunne; features Lionel Barrymore, Van Johnson, James Gleason, Ward Bond, Barry Nelson. Directed by Victor Fleming. Screenplay, Dalton Trumbo, adaptation by Frederick Hazlitt Brennan from original story by Major Chandler Sprague and David Boehm; editor, Frederick Brennan; camera (b&w), George Folsey, Karl Freund. Reviewed at Capitol theatre, New York, Dec. 23, '43. Running Time: 120 Mins.

Pete Sandidge	Spencer Tracy
Dorinda Durston	Irene Dunne
Ted Randall	Van Johnson
Al Yackey	Ward Bond
Nails Kilpatrick	James Gleason
The General	Lionel Barrymore
Dick Rumney	Barry Nelson
Ellen Bright	Esther Williams
Colonel Sykes	Henry O'Neill
James J. Rourke.	Don DeFore
Sanderson	Charles Smith

Not quite the transcendent adult love story one might have hoped to find Spielberg capable of at this point in his

career, "Always" has a predominantly goofy, adolescent tone. Dreyfuss' debonair approach and the delightful antics of his sidekick pilot John Goodman (in the old Ward Bond part) help keep the film from getting maudlin.

Stepping into Tracy's shoes without strain, Dreyfuss has a similar kind of amiability and kindliness, a gentlemanly ease with women that is unusual in today's films. His ghostly dance with Hunter is one of the film's most touching scenes.

Spielberg is not so successful with Johnson, who has the square-jawed good looks of a comic-book character. But with his terrible John Wayne impressions, oafish courting behaviour and dimwitted expressions, he comes off the male equivalent of a dumb blond with a great figure.

Among the superlative tech credits are Mikael Salomon's lensing, Michael Kahn's editing, James Bissell's production design, Bruce Nicholson's supervision of the Industrial Light & Magic visual effects, and Mike Wood's supervision of the forest fire special effects.

John Williams' music is rousing, and Spielberg wittily substitutes "Smoke Gets In Your Eyes" for "I'll Get By" as the couple's theme music. It's a shame that the haunting melody from Irving Berlin's "Always," which would have been so appropriate here, reportedly was denied to Spielberg.

Mac.

HOOK

December 9, 1991

A Tri-Star release of an Amblin Entertainment production. Produced by Kathleen Kennedy, Frank Marshall, Gerald R. Molen. Executive producers, Dodi Fayed, Jim V. Hart. Co-producers, Gary Adelson, Craig Baumgarten. Directed by Steven Spielberg. Screenplay, Hart, Malia Scotch Marmo, screen story by Hart, Nick Castle, based on J.M. Barrie's original stageplay and books. Camera (Deluxe color; Deluxe and Technicolor prints; Panavision widescreen), Dean Cundey; editor, Michael Kahn; music, John Williams; production design, Norman Garwood; visual consultant, John Napier; art direction, Andrew Precht, Thomas E. Sanders; set design Henry Alberti, Thomas Betts, Joseph Hodges, Peter J. Kelly, Joseph G. Pacelli Jr., Jacques Valin; set decoration, Garrett Lewis; costume design, Anthony Powell; special visual effects, Industrial Light & Magic; visual effects supervisor, Eric Brevig; special effects supervisor, Michael Lantieri; stunt coordinator-action choreographer, Gary Hymes; choreographer, Vince Paterson; special makeup, Greg Cannom; associate producers, Bruce cohen, Marmo; assistant director, Cohen; casting, Janet Hirshenson, Jane Jenkins, Michael Hirshenson. Reviewed at Avco Cinema, L.A., Dec. 4, 1991. MPAA Rating: PG. Running time: 144 Mins.

Captain Hook	Dustin Hoffman
Peter Banning/Peter Pan	Robin Williams
Tinkerbell	Julia Roberts
Smee	Bob Hoskins
Granny Wendy	Maggie Smith
Moira	Caroline Goodall
Jack	Charlie Korsmo
Maggie	Amber Scott
Liza	Laurel Cronin
Inspector Good	Phil Collins
Tootles	Arthur Malet
Pockets	Isaiah Robinson
Ace	Jasen Fisher
Rufio	Dante Basco
Thud Butt	Raushan Hammond
Don't Ask	James Madio
Too Small	Thomas Tulak
Latchboy	Alex Zuckerman
No Nap	Ahmad Stoner

"Hook" feels as much like a massive amusement park ride as it does a film. Spirited, rambunctious, often messy and undisciplined, this determined attempt to recast the Peter Pan story in contempo terms splashes every bit of its megabudget (between $60 million and $80 million) onto the screen; commercial elements overflow in such abundance that major hit status seems guaranteed.

A shade sophisticated for small kids and too indulgent for more demanding adults, pic will find favor with mainstream audiences without, perhaps, being taken deeply to heart: The "E.T."-like magic doesn't click in, but it will certainly be one of the three or four biggest films of the year.

Often called a Peter Pan himself for his unparalleled ability to capture the innocent wonder of childhood in his films, Steven Spielberg has long wanted to put some version of the classic J.M. Barrie tale on the big screen. He found his way in with Jim V. Hart's screenplay, which, as amended by co-writer Malia Scotch Marmo, sends a modern, grown-up Peter, a man who has forgotten his youth, back to Neverland to rescue his children from the clutches of the ever-vengeful Captain Hook.

Material could scarcely be more pregnant with thematic possibilities for Spielberg, who has so often favored kids' p.o.v. over that of adults, and is now roughly the same age as the hero of the picture. His basic proposition is that to enter the state of mind where anything is possible, one must reawaken the child inside.

Setup is deftly done, sweeping the viewer right into world of the Banning family. Peter (Robin Williams) is a workaholic corporate attorney so busy he sends an underling to videotape his son's Little League games. But he manages to tear himself away to take his wife Moira (Caroline Goodall) and Children Jack (Charlie Korsmo) and Maggie (Amber Scott) to London to visit Granny Wendy (Maggie Smith).

Back in Blighty, Jack and Maggie are spirited away, courtesy Captain James Hook. Mystified, Peter is visited by Tinkerbell (Julia Roberts) and, 36 minutes into the story, is transported to Neverland, where Hook (Dustin Hoffman) lords over a raucous Pirate Town from the deck of his enormous ship.

Humiliated by Hook, Peter is granted three days to prepare for his battle with the eager captain, who has been waiting ages for his rematch with the follow responsible for his losing his hand to a crocodile. Woefully out of shape and still unaware of his previous identity, Peter is thrown in with the Lost Boys, Peter Pan's errant tribe of orphans who look askance at this pretender to their leadership.

Sweet and likable through the first half-hour, pic becomes dominated by a vaude-ville tone and in-jokes during the pirate section (Glenn Close turns up in male disguise as a sailor victimized by Hook), and slides into environmental theme park hijinks once it reaches the boys' playground.

Devised by production designer Norman Garwood and visual consultant John Napier (and revealing the strong influence of the latter's stage designs for "Cats," "Les Miserables" and "Starlight Express") spectacular set is replete with tram tracks, vines, water holes, a tree-house, all of which are enthusiastically used by boys of all ethnic persuasions and tough attitudes, but which also emphasize the theatricality of the proceedings.

But a little of this stuff goes a long way, and pic's middle portion sags

considerably as Peter's oafish efforts to recapture his former self are intercut with Hook's devilish and initially successful attempt to win the love of young Jack and convince him that Peter is a bad father.

Finally, after 97 minutes, Peter becomes "the Pan," taking wing in tech-nically impeccable flying sequences and assuming definitive leadership of the Lost Boys. Despite the cascade of won-drous special effects, massive battles between the kids and pirates and face-offs between Pan and Hook, the film doesn't truly take flight, as it vigorously but mechanically works through several climaxes before settling back in London for the inevitable family reunion.

The sheer inventiveness and quantity of diverting elements make for a reason-able degree of entertainment value, but Spielberg lets it sprawl on for too long. Much of the action in the campground seems aimless and visually unfocused. Clearly engaged in working out the psychological, mythic and thematic aspects of the story, director loses his grip on concise storytelling and dramatic punch, sacrificing any suspense (which the original had) in the process.

Stature of the title character has also been reduced in this rendition, as joki-ness gets the better of both Hoffman, who brandishes an erratic British accent and barely conceals the method of his badness, and Bob Hoskins, who plays the captain's loyal hand, Smee, with customary relish but little genuine humor.

Dialogue throughout has its share of snappy zingers, and elements from Barrie's original works are cleverly incor-porated, but neither actor is furnished with sterling material that can quite match their abilities to put it across.

Williams was the most natural choice to play this resurgent Pan, and he inhab-its the role splendidly. Properly uptight as the lawyer and absent father, he becomes an utterly convincing leader to his band of kids, and is a Peter Pan any viewer can believe in (although some with recent memories of "The Fisher King" will be amused at how he has shaved off his body hair for this role).

Playing scenes mostly alone or miniaturized opposite a looming Williams, Roberts makes a beguiling, leggy Tinkerbell, and Charlie Korsmo, remembered from "Dick Tracy," is fine as Peter's son who falls under Hook's spell.

But the standout supporting turns come from Smith, perfect as the aged Wendy, and Goodall, who transforms the potentially sticky role of Peter's wife into a beautiful miniature portrait of motherly love and devotion, with the best speech of the show.

Rockers Phil Collins and David Crosby pop up in bits, but there's no sign of Michael Jackson or Bruce Willis, both rumored during production to have been slipped into the cast.

Spielberg's theme of retaining youthful sense of wonder, playfulness and imagination carries plenty of resonance, and seems notably directed to materialists among his baby boomer generation. But it's so emphatically stated as to be less than entirely moving.

Pic is unquestionably one of the most stupendous productions ever mounted on soundstages. Surrounded by a cyclorama and lit from artificial sources, the Neverland sets provide constant distraction. The same goes for the costumes, makeup, stunts and special effects all of which are as good as they get.

Dean Cundey's lensing glows in the opening and closing sections; Michael Kahn's editing is fluid and propulsive as always, while John Williams' ever-present score lays it on a bit thick this time.

Biggest laugh at the L.A. press screening came when Peter takes his family to London, and a stock airplane shot shows them travelling by Pan Am, which ceased operations the same day.

Todd McCarthy

JURASSIC PARK

June 14, 1993

A Universal release of an Amblin Entertainment production. Produced by Kathleen Kennedy, Gerald R. Molen. Directed by Steven Spielberg. Screenplay, Michael Crichton, David Koepp, from Crichton's novel. Camera (Deluxe color), Dean Cundey; editor, Michael Kahn; music, John Williams; production design, Rick Carter; art direction, Jim Teegarden, John Bell; set design, John Berger, Lauren Polizzi, Masako Masuda; set decoration, Jackie Carr; sound (Dolby; The Digital Experience), Ron Judkins; sound design, Gary Rydstrom; full-motion dinosaurs, Dennis Muren; live-action dinosaurs, Stan Winston; dinosaur supervisor, Phil Tippett, special dinosaur effects, Michael Lantieri; full-motion dinosaurs and special visual effects, Industrial Light & Magic; stunt coordinator, Gary Hymes; associate producers, Lata Ryan, Colin Wilson; assistant director, John T. Kretchmer; aerial unit director, David Nowell; "Mr. D.N.A." animation, Kirtz and Friends; casting, Janet Hirshenson, Jane Jenkins. Reviewed at Universal Studios, Universal City, Calif., June 2, 1993. MPAA Rating: PG-13. Running time: 126 Mins.

Dr. Alan Grant	Sam Neill
Ellie Sattler	Laura Dern
Ian Malcolm	Jeff Goldblum
John Hammond	Richard Attenborough
Robert Muldoon	Bob Peck
Donald Gennaro	Martin Ferrero
Dr. Wu	B.D. Wong
Tim	Joseph Mazzello
Lex	Ariana Richards
Arnold	Samuel L. Jackson
Dennis Nedry	Wayne Knight
Park Tour Voice	Richard Kiley

"Jurassic Park" will at least disabuse anyone of the idea that it would be fun to share the planet with dinosaurs. Steven Spielberg's scary and horrific thriller may be one-dimensional and even clunky in story and characterization, but definitely delivers where it counts, in excitement, suspense and the stupendous realization of giant reptiles. Having finally found another set of "Jaws" worthy of the name, Spielberg and Universal have a monster hit on their hands.

Very cleverly, the film positions itself both as a dark look at a theme park gone awry, and as a theme park itself. Merchandising, Universal tour attractions and sequels will extend the profits enormously. The only thing that will keep this properly PG-13-rated extravaganza from approaching rarefied "Star Wars" and "E.T." b.o. heights is its inappropriateness for kids under 10 or 12 – it's just too intense.

The $60 million production (a bargain at the price) follows the general idea if not the letter of co-scriptor Michael Crichton's 1990 bestseller.

Basis of this hi-tech, scientifically based, up-to-date version lies in the notion that living, breathing and eating full-sized dinosaurs can be biologically engineered using fossilized dino D.N.A. Having accomplished this in secret on an island off Costa Rica, zillionaire entrepreneur/tycoon John Hammond (Richard Attenborough) brings in a small group of experts to view and, he hopes, endorse his miracle, which is to be the world's most expensive zoo-cum-amusement park.

Arriving to inspect the menagerie are paleontologists Dr. Alan Grant (Sam Neill) and Ellie Sattler (Laura Dern), as well as oddball mathematician Ian Malcolm (Jeff Goldblum), advocate of the Chaos Theory, a sort of numerical equivalent of Murphy's Law. Also along for the look-see are Donald Gennaro (Martin Ferrero), a hard-nosed attorney repping the park's investors, and Hammond's two fresh-faced grandchildren, Lex (Ariana Richards) and Tim (Joseph Mazzello).

Introductory scenes are surprisingly perfunctory and even sloppy, as there are several bad cuts unworthy of a filmmaker of Spielberg's skill, and the script wouldn't pass muster in Screenwriting 101. Equally surprisingly, Spielberg lets the dinosaurs out of the bag very early, showing some of them in full view after only 20 minutes.

Still, none of these problems ends up mattering once the film clicks into high gear. When a storm strands two carloads of Hammond's guests in the middle of the park at night, a Tyrannosaurus rex decides it's dinner-time. Suddenly, after a fitful first hour, Spielberg pulls off one of the most exciting set pieces of his career, highlighted by a stunning shot of a T-Rex in a rear view mirror and climaxed by a gag lifted from Buster Keaton's "Steamboat Bill Jr."

Events from here on frighteningly verify the mathematician's view of an unpredictable universe. With command central's computer and power system shut down, the dinosaurs are free to run amok, thanks to the treachery of rotund hacker Dennis Nedry (Wayne Knight).

Grant and the two kids are forced to make their way back across the park to the compound, and their adventures are spiked by arguably the most beautiful and awe-inspiring scene in the film, in which a herd of speedy small dinosaurs sweep towards the characters across a plain and away from a hungry T-Rex, who ultimately enjoys a meal. The outdoor perspectives here, after a nocturnal studio work, prove particularly refreshing. The reptiles here are brilliantly convincing – lifelike, crafty, smooth of movement and numerous. Taking special bows in this department are special effects wizards Stan Winston, Dennis Muren, Phil Tippett, Michael Lantieri and hundreds of technicians, at Industrial Light & Magic and elsewhere.

In fact, the monsters are far more convincing than the human characters. Saddled with skin-deep roles, the actors are not in much of a position to distinguish themselves. Sam Neill's paleontologist comes off rather like a bland Indiana Jones, while Laura Dern considerably overdoes the facial oohs and ahhs. The kids are basically along for the ride, while Jeff Goldblum, attired in all-black, helpfully fires off most of the wisecracks.

As for Richard Attenborough, agreeably back onscreen for the first time since 1979, his role has been significantly softened from the book, turned from single-mindedly malevolent developer into a profit-minded grandpa willing to acknowledge his folly.

While the gore of the novel has been toned down to unbloody levels, and the body count is notably lower (as if with the wave of a hand, the vast number of workers at the park are made to disappear when convenient), Spielberg nevertheless turns the screws very tight in the film's second hour, having evidently decided to sacrifice the youngest potential viewers in order to give everyone else a good scare.

Technically, the film is sometimes more than it needs to be. As in some of Spielberg's previous outings, Dean Cundey's lensing overdoes the back illumination and shafts of light at times, and John Williams' score gets unnecessarily bombastic. But the dinosaurs rule here, and Spielberg and his team of special effects aces have put something on the screen that people have never seen before, which is the surest way to create a blockbuster.

Todd McCarthy

SCHINDLER'S LIST

December 13, 1993

'Schindler' makes A-list

A Universal release of an Amblin Entertainment production. Produced by Steven Spielberg, Gerald R. Molen, Branko Lustig. Executive producer, Kathleen Kennedy. Co-producer, Lew Rywin. Directed by Spielberg. Screenplay, Steven Zaillian, based on the novel by Thomas Keneally. Camera (b&w, Deluxe prints), Janusz Kaminski; editor, Michael Kahn; music, John Williams; violin solos, Itzhak Perlman; production design, Allan Starski; art direction, Ewa Sckoczkowska, Maciej Walczak, Ewa Tarnowska, Ryszard Melliwa, Grzegorz Piatkowski; set decoration, Ewa Braun; costume design, Anna Biedrzycka-Sheppard; sound, Ronald Judkins, Robert Jackson; associate producers, Irving Glovin, Robert Raymond; assistant directors, Sergio Mimica-Gezzan, Marek Brodzki (Poland); casting, Lucky Englander, Fritz Fleischhacker, Magdalena Szwarchart, Tova Cypin, Liat Meiron, Juliet Taylor. Reviewed at Universal Studios, Universal city, Nov. 18, 1993. MPAA Rating: R. Running time: 195 Mins.

Oskar Schindler	Liam Neeson
Itzhak Stern	Ben Kingsley
Amon Goeth	Ralph Fiennes
Emilie Schindler	Caroline Goodall
Poldek Pfefferberg	Jonathan Sagalle
Helen Hirsch	Embeth Davidtz

After several attempts at making a fully realized, mature film, Steven Spielberg has finally put it all together in "Schindler's List." A remarkable work by any standard, this searing historical and biographical drama, about a Nazi industrialist who saved some 1,100 Jews from certain death in the concentration camps, evinces an artistic rigor and unsentimental intelligence unlike anything the world's most successful filmmaker has demonstrated before. Marked by a brilliant screenplay, exceptionally supple technique, three staggeringly good lead performances and an attitude towards the traumatic subject matter that is both passionately felt and impressively restrained, this is the film to win over Spielberg's skeptics.

How the general public will take to a three-hour, fifteen-minute, black-and-white epic about the Holocaust with no major stars is another matter. Even with the cards of conventional wisdom stacked against it, top reviews, off-entertainment page coverage, possible awards and the Spielberg name should stir enough interest to turn release into an event, elevating it to must-see status for discerning audiences worldwide. The gamble should pay off financially as well as artistically.

Besides being familiar, the Nazi persecution of the Jews is perilous subject matter since it can so easily elicit automatic reactions of moral outrage, personal horror, religious self-righteousness and dramatic extremes, not to mention severe depression.

Taking their cue from Australian writer Thomas Keneally's 1982 book of the same name, Spielberg and scenarist Stephen Zaillian have overcome the problem of familiarity by presenting innumerable details of this grim history that are utterly fresh and previously unexplored, at least in mainstream films. And they have triumphed over the most obvious potential pitfalls by keeping as their main focus a man whose mercenary instincts only gradually turned him into an unlikely hero and saviour.

Oskar Schindler (the imposing, impeccably groomed Liam Neeson) is masterfully introduced in a rowdy nightclub sequence that instantly builds interest and mystique around him as he curries favor with the Nazis, who have completed their lightning conquest of Poland in September 1939.

With Jews being registered and entering Krakow at the rate of 10,000 per week, Nazi Party member Schindler arranges to run a major company that will be staffed by unpaid Jews. Itzhak Stern (Ben Kingsley) becomes his accountant and right-hand man and helps build the concern into a major supplier of pots, pans and cookware for troops at the front.

In near-documentary fashion and often using a dizzyingly mobile, hand-held camera, Spielberg (who operates his own camera for many of these sequences) deftly sketches the descent of the Jews from refugee settlers in Krakow to their confinement within 16 square blocks by 1941, to the creation of a Plaszow Forced Labor Camp in 1942, to the brutal liquidation of the ghetto the following year. In fascinating detail, and using a plethora of vivid characters, the film shows how the black market worked, how previously well-to-do families were forced into miserable dwellings, how the *Judenrat* – Jews nominally empowered by the Germans – oversaw and carried out Nazi law, how some managed to survive and others didn't.

In these sequences, the seed is planted for one of the picture's superbly developed great themes – that the matter of who lived and died was completely, utterly, existentially arbitrary. As one of the characters observes, the casualness and randomness of Nazi cruelty was such that at no point could one develop a strategy for survival; there was no safe way to behave, and even extreme cleverness couldn't save you in the long run. All morality, justice and personal worth was erased.

With the clearing of Krakow, most of the action shifts to the labor camp, which is set in an extraordinary location at the base of a cliff. Looming above it is the opulent chateau of Commandant Amon

Goeth (Ralph Fiennes), from which invited revelers can look down upon the prisoners during glittering parties and, in shocking scenes that, again, are unlike anything previously seen, from the balcony of which the commandant randomly shoots helpless inmates as if taking target practice.

The commandant is a fascinating creation, as evil as any Nazi presented onscreen over the past 50 years, but considerably more complex and human than most. He is deeply and, he admits, disturbingly attracted to the young Jewish woman he keeps as his personal maid. Tellingly, both he and Schindler drink a great deal, but Goeth admires Schindler for not, unlike him, being a drunk. "That's control," he says, "and control is power."

Schindler must use utmost diplomacy in dealing with Goeth and other top-ranking Nazis in order to get his way, gently suggesting that their murderous policies are bad for business and that to bestow a pardon confers even greater power on a ruler than constantly meting out death. Schindler is permitted to continue operating his Krakow factory as a "sub-camp," which becomes a virtual haven for hundreds of Jews in that they are basically assured they won't die there.

Still, with the Final Solution being implemented with ever-greater dispatch by 1944, Schindler must finally buy, with his tremendous war profits, the leftover Jews to prevent them from being shipped to Auschwitz. In a harrowing sequence, women he has arranged to rescue wind up at the extermination camp by mistake. For Schindler as well as the Jews, it remains a question of which will last longer, his money or the war.

After listening to Churchill's announcement of the German surrender, Schindler delivers an extraordinary speech of his own in the presence of both Nazi guards and Jewish workers before fleeing with nothing more than a suitcase. Throughout the mesmerizing narrative so masterfully orchestrated in Zaillian's faultlessly intelligent screenplay, there are many opportunities for heart-tugging, obvious plays for sympathy and hate, maudlin sentiments and cheap indulgences. Not only because Spielberg resisted every one of them, but also because his film is so different, and so much tougher, than anything else he's done, if not forewarned as to its director's identity, even a well-schooled critic could watch virtually the entire picture and never suspect it was Spielberg.

On reflection, some of the themes relating to greed, corruption and inadvertent heroism have been present in his work from early on, but nothing before has been anywhere near this deep or resonant. Images, moments and scenes stay in the mind and become even stronger, well after viewing the film.

Despite its 3 1/4 hour length, the film moves forward with great urgency and is not a minute too long for the story it is telling and the amount of information it imparts. It is, naturally, full of violence and death, but Spielberg makes this both memorable and somehow bearable by staging it all with abrupt, shocking suddenness, which adds to the feeling of arbitrariness.

This is not, strictly speaking, a concentration camp movie but a densely woven personal drama with the most striking of historical backdrops, which is what will get mainstream audiences through it.

The only debatable choice is the brief color epilogue, which depicts many of the surviving "Schindler Jews" filing by his grave in Israel accompanied, for the most part, by the much younger actors who have portrayed them in the film. This will have many viewers crying their eyes out, but it also smacks, on a certain level, of direct emotional manipulation, the only such instance in the work.

Another device that uses color is also questionable, that of a little girl whom Schindler notices and whose red coat stands out against the prevailing black-and-white. What this is supposed to signify is anyone's guess, although it's so minor that it doesn't matter.

From top to bottom, the performances from the enormous cast are impeccable. Whereas the most major stars would have wanted to tip the audience off early on that Schindler was actually a sensitive, caring guy underneath it all, Neeson leaves no doubt through most of the film that his character was driven foremost by profit. In a superlative performance, Neeson makes Schindler a fascinating but highly ambiguous figure, effectively persuasive and manipulative in one-on-one scenes where he's determined to get what he wants, and finally rising to dramatic heights with his courageous and stirring farewell speech.

Kingsley must act within much more rigid constraints as his trusted accountant Stern, a man who feels he must never make a misstep. Role is reminiscent of Alec Guinness' deluded Col. Nicholson in "The Bridge on the River Kwai"; in his compulsion to do a perfect job for Schindler, he often seems to forget that he's working for the enemy.

The extraordinary Fiennes creates an indelible charter in Goeth. With paunch hanging out and eyes filled with disgust both for his victims and himself, he's like a minor-league Roman emperor gone sour with excess, a man in whom too much power and debauchery have crushed anything that might once have been good.

The dozens of small roles, many of which figure in the action only briefly, have been superbly filled by faces that invariably register immediately and with terrific effectiveness.

Shot mostly on location in Poland, the picture captures in exceptional detail the nightmare world of 50 years ago. Allan Starski's production detail blends imperceptibly with natural locations. This is a film that could have been made only in black-and-white, and yet it is solely because of Spielberg's commercial stature that it was able to be made that way. Lensing by Janusz Kaminski, a young Polish-American cinematographer whose previous credits include "The Adventures of Huck Finn," Diane Keaton's made-for-cable "Wildflower" and some Roger Corman efforts, is outstanding. Lighting is mostly very simple, camera moves are agile and perceptive, and palette features many shades of gray rather than high-contrast black-and-white.

Michael Kahn's editing moves with dynamic swiftness when desired and holds on scenes when required, making the running time seem shorter. John Williams' score is atypical, especially in the context of his work for Spielberg, as it's low-key, soulful and flecked with ethnic flavors.

Dedicated to the late Time Warner chairman Steve Ross, "Schindler's List" has a deep emotional impact that is extraordinarily well served and balanced by its intelligence, historical perspective and filmmaking expertise.

Todd McCarthy

THE LOST WORLD JURASSIC PARK

May 19–25, 1997

'Lost' in a world of visual thrills

A Universal Films release of an Amblin Entertainment production. Produced by Gerald Molen, Colin Wilson. Executive producer, Kathleen Kennedy. Directed by Steven Spielberg. Screenplay, David Koepp, based on the novel by Michael Crichton. Camera (Deluxe color), Janusz Kaminski; editor, Michael Kahn; music, John Williams; production design, Rick Carter; art direction, Jim Teegarden; set design, Pamela Klamer, Linda King; costume supervisor, Sue Moore; sound (DTS Digital, stereo), Ron Judkins, Robert Jackson; full-motion dinosaurs, Dennis Muren; live-action dinosaurs, Stan Winston; special dinosaur effects, Michael Lantieri; stunt coordinators, M. James Arnett, Gary Hymes; assistant director, Sergio Mimica-Gezzan; second unit director, Koepp; casting, Janet Hirshenson, Jane Jenkins. Reviewed at Universal Studios, Universal City, May 15, 1997. MPAA Rating: PG-13. Running time: 134 Mins.

Dr. Ian Malcolm	Jeff Goldblum
Dr. Sarah Harding	Julianne Moore
Roland Tembo	Pete Postlethwaite
Peter Ludlow	Arliss Howard
John Hammond	Richard Attenborough
Nick Van Owen	Vince Vaughn
Kelly Curtis	Vanessa Lee Chester
Dieter Stark	Peter Stormare
Ajay Sidhu	Harvey Jason
Eddie Carr	Richard Schiff
Dr. Robert Burke	Thomas F. Duffy
Tim	Joseph Mazzello
Lex	Ariana Richards

Following up on the highest-grossing film of all time was bound to be a daunting task. The good news about 'The Lost World: Jurassic Park" is that the dinosaur creations are even better than those in the first film, credible, breathtaking and frightening. As for the rest, every department pales by comparison. Still, the film provides sufficient visceral thrills and visual delights to engage audiences and rack up bronto grosses. It remains the picture most likely to succeed this summer, even if Universal and Amblin will have to settle for somewhat diminished returns.

The premise is that 80 miles from the original "Jurassic Park," there was Site B, the island locale where the prehistoric animals were engineered and shipped off to the filed theme park. and as the amusement attraction was being undone by man, the scientific base was destroyed by a hurricane.

Though it was presumed the dinos died for want of a life-giving chemical, they found the element in nature and have been thriving unmonitored ever since. In the words of mastermind John Hammond (Richard Attenborough), "life will find a way."

The idea now is to send in a small expedition to chronicle the progress. The quartet is composed of documentarian Nick Van Owen (Vince Vaughn), operations specialist Eddie Carr (Richard Schiff), paleontologist Sarah Harding (Julianne Moore) and reluctant returnee Ian Malcolm (Jeff Goldblum). Malcolm agrees only because he recognizes the lurking danger and hopes to get girlfriend Harding off the island as quickly as possible.

The arrival of Site B is a reminder of what made "Jurassic Park" so memorable. The seamless interplay between modern man and extinct creatures is pure magic. But as with first pic, any sense of serenity is short-lived. First, Malcolm's daughter, Kelly (Vanessa Lee Chester), is discovered having stowed away on the expedition. Then a second, much larger, team descends from the skies for less honorable pursuits. Led by Hammond nephew and corporate chief Peter Ludlow (Arliss Howard), this crew of mercenaries is on a mission to capture a selection of bygone species for display in a new San Diego park.

It doesn't take long for the tables to turn. Soon, the hunters become the prey and both groups have to join forces and wiles to ensure their return to civilization. Along the way their ranks are seriously depleted by the likes of Raptors and Tyrannosaurus Rexes.

David Koepp's script, from the Michael Crichton novel, is schematic and largely predictable. There's an obvious threat and not too many ways to quell it. Underneath the technical virtuosity is a standard chase film, and director Steven Spielberg does little to elevate it dramatically. His skill at making the audience jump at the appropriate moment is nonetheless intact, and in the absence of a strong story and well-delineated characters, that's a mighty important asset.

The cast mostly founders with sketchily written parts. Goldblum, elevated from foil to leading man, is given double duty as hero and comic relief. He simply isn't provided with the ammunition to anchor the film. Moore and Howard are also saddled with thankless, archetypal roles. Only Vaughn and Pete Postlethwaite – as a big-game hunter with a passion to go toe-to-toe with a T-Rex – rise above the material's limitations. The most textured performance may indeed come from a matriarchal carnivore who'll stop at nothing to protect her youngster.

While pic is slickly produced, Janusz Kaminski's photography seems rather self-consciously arty for the genre. It's rife with back-lighting to accentuate the eeriness of night and fog. Otherwise, the film moves at a breathless clip that almost makes one forget the thinness of the plot.

Few filmmakers have been able to replicate the success and artistry of an all-time popular hit in a sequel. There's simply too much baggage and anticipation. What's surprising about "The Lost World" is an almost slavish duplication of horror conventions of the past, including many from the Spielberg canon. An unquestionably potent formula, it nonetheless evaporates quickly because of its reliance on manipulation. One gets a queasy feeling, for instance, about making Malcolm's daughter a mulatto. Is it a sincere statement or demographically inspired?

In the rear-view mirror the picture is calculation at the expense of inspiration. There's no question that all the right buttons are hit by a master craftsman. Like popcorn, it's a tasty, fun ride without a great deal of nutritional value.

Leonard Klady

AMISTAD

December 8–14, 1997

Spielberg's chronicle of social justice

A DreamWorks Picture release in association with HBO Pictures. Produced by Steven Spielberg, Debbie Allen, Colin Wilson. Executive producers, Walter Parks, Laurie MacDonald. Co-executive producer, Robert Cooper. Co-producer, Tim Shriver. Directed by Steven Spielberg. Screenplay, David Franzoni. Camera (Technicolor, widescreen), Janusz Kaminski; editor, Michael Kahn; music, John Williams; production design, Rick Carter; art direction, Chris Burian-Mohr, Jim Teegarden, Tony Fanning; set decoration, Rosemary Brandenburg; costume design, Ruth E. Carter, sound (Delby/DTS/SDDS), Ronald Judkins, Robert Jackson; visual effects, Industrial Light & Magic; visual effects supervisor, Scott Farrar; associate producers, Bonnie Curtis, Paul Deason; assistant director, Sergio Mimica-Gezzan; casting, Victoria Thomas. Reviewed at Amblin Entertainment, Universal City, Nov. 28, 1997. MPAA Rating: R. Running time: 152 Mins.

Theodore Joadson	Morgan Freeman
John Quincy Adams	Anthony Hopkins
Baldwin	Matthew McConaughey
Martin Van Buren	Nigel Hawthorne
Cinque	Djimon Hounsou
Secretary Forsyth	David Paymer
Holabird	Pete Postlethwaite
Tappan.	Stellan Skarsgard
Queen Isabella	Anna Paquin
Calderon	Tomas Milian
Professor Gibbs	Austin Pendleton

The forces of power, racism and justice momentously clash in Steven Spielberg's "Amistad," an artistically solid, if not always dramatically exciting, chronicle of the 1839 rebellion on board the Spanish slave ship of the title. True story, which few Americans have ever heard about, is presented as an international intrigue of a high order, one that involved the governments of pre-Civil War U.S., Great Britain, Spain and, of course, the 53 Africans held captive in the cramped cargo off the Cuban coast. Boasting a high-voltage cast, led by Brits Anthony Hopkins and Nigel Hawthorne, Americans Morgan Freeman and Matthew McConaughey and, most impressively, West African Djimon Hounsou as the rebels' leader, this second release from DreamWorks should sail safely as a message film that touches on the very fabric of the American social system.

Spielberg's second foray into African-American history is far more effective and moving than "The Color Purple," his compromised, sanitized rendition of Alice Walker's novel. Thematically, the new film is a logical endeavor following "Schindler's List," though stylistically the two films are very different. Aiming to instruct as well as entertain – and often struggling to reconcile these two divergent goals — "Amistad" lacks the subtlety of tone and simplicity of form that made the 1993 Oscar-winning film so special in Spielberg's oeuvre.

The director strives a tad too hard to emphasize the universal elements of the 19th-century case of injustice, using a deliberate visual style that accentuates (and often inflates) every idea and image. Spielberg skeptics will find ammunition to criticize "Amistad" as too solemnly earnest and too bombastic in its visual strategy.

In a powerful pre-credits sequence that evidences a conspicuously bold touch, Spielberg shows how Sengbe Pieh (called Cinque by the Spaniards) begins the rebellion when he breaks free of his shackles. This violent scene (partly responsible for pic's R rating) depicts graphically, with mega-close-ups and rapid montage, the impalement of an officer on a sword.

From this point on, David Franzoni's multifaceted script relates the saga from the perspective of its central victim, a once-free rice farmer who suddenly found himself a chained slave. With Cinque (Hounsou), the filmmakers provide the audience a most sympathetic figure – and an emotional hook – to absorb the sprawling drama as it hops from one continent to another.

After the rebels are caught and thrown into a New England prison, story switches to Theodore Joadson (Freeman), a former slave who has joined forces with a businessman called Tappan (Stellan Skarsgard) in the abolitionist cause. When the Amistad incident breaks, the American press labels it "a massacre at sea," but Joadson perceives the Africans as freedom fighters. Attempting to enlist a decent attorney, he ends up with Baldwin (McConaughey), a shady property lawyer nicknamed "Dung Scraper."

For Baldwin, the case represents a property, not a human rights, issue. Indeed, in the trial, positioned against Holabird (Pete Postlethwaite), the nasty government prosecutor, Baldwin tries desperately to prove that the Africans were not legally slaves, that they were "stolen goods" because they were born in Africa and illegally kidnapped from their homes.

Drama becomes intriguingly complex when broader political forces are brought to the surface. Fearing the wrath of the South, President Martin Van Buren (Hawthorne), who's running for re-election, overturns the lower court's decision, which had favored the Africans. He and his secretary of state, Forsyth (David Paymer), shamelessly pull strings behind the scenes and even appoint a new attorney.

The case goes to the Supreme Court, where the Africans are defended by none other than John Quincy Adams (Hopkins), the former president and son of founding father John Adams.

Neither an abolitionist nor pro-slavery, Adams is a reluctant hero, an astute, incorruptible puritan, enamored of flowers and plants, who initially refuses to help. A moralist at heart, he throws himself wholeheartedly into defending the Africans in a fervent speech that summons the Declaration of Independence and other tenets of the American Dream.

Looking at the case, from a contempo p.o.v., the script contains some astutely cynical observations about politicians, as when one official says, "Is there anything more pathetic than an ex-president?" The statement refers to Adams, but will have resonance for present-day viewers. All along there are jokes about Spain's Queen Isabella (Anna Paquin), a pubescent still playing with dolls, who later continued to argue about the Amistad case with seven presidents.

Though there are a number of trials, Spielberg shrewdly avoids the routine format of courtroom drama, instead seamlessly integrating the numerous characters and their particular stands on the case. Yet every once in a while one senses an inner tension between Spielberg the mass entertainer, with his assured command of camera and trademark pyrotechnics and the genuine artist, pressing for the simple core of the drama.

Occasionally, the film succumbs to the level of anthropological survey, viewing the Africans and their rituals as exotic curiosity, though Hounsou's dignified portrayal of Cinque as a man of outer strength and inner peace successfully counters this weakness. Regrettably, the always brilliant Freeman is totally wasted as Joadson, functioning as no more than a link among the various episodes, a possible result of the fact that his fictional character is a composite of several historical figures.

Cast against type, with shabby beard

and big glasses to deglamorize his handsomeness, McConaughey renders a passable performance, failing to grab the opportunities of his substantial role. Playing a man older than his age, Hopkins shines throughout, and once he takes center stage he ignites the screen with a bravura 11-minute argument that results in the freeing of the slaves and crushing of the notorious Lomboka Slave Fortress.

The large, inspired ensemble hits its marks with small but succinctly drawn roles, with Hawthorne as the pro-slavery present, Paymer as the cunning secretary of state and Skarsgard as the decent abolitionist, among others.

Filmed in various locations in New England and Puerto Rico, technically "Amistad" is an aural and visual pleasure, due to John Williams' emotional score, Janusz Kaminski's vibrant lensing, Rick Carter's accurate production design and Ruth Carter's historically genuine costumes all contributing to an authentic experience, which is further enhanced by the Africans' use of the Mende language.

Emanuel Levy

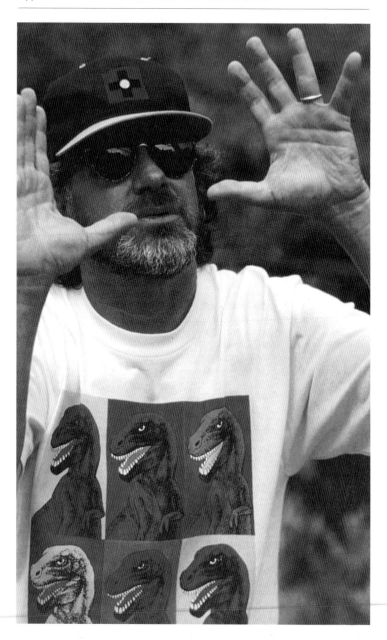